Starting from Loomis

The George and Sakaye Aratani Nikkei in the Americas Series
Series editor Lane Hirabayashi

This series endeavors to capture the best available scholarship illustrating the evolving nature of contemporary Japanese American culture and community. By stretching the boundaries of the field to the limit (whether at a substantive, theoretical, or comparative level) these books aspire to influence future scholarship in this area specifically and Asian American Studies more generally.

The House on Lemon Street, Mark Howland Rawitsch

Starting from Loomis and Other Stories, Hiroshi Kashiwagi,
edited and with an introduction by Tim Yamamura

Starting
from
Loomis

and
Other
Stories

HIROSHI KASHIWAGI

EDITED WITH AN
INTRODUCTION BY
TIM YAMAMURA

AFTERWORD BY
LANE RYO HIRABAYASHI

UNIVERSITY PRESS OF COLORADO
Boulder

© 2013 by University Press of Colorado

Published by University Press of Colorado
5589 Arapahoe Avenue, Suite 206C
Boulder, Colorado 80303

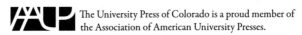 The University Press of Colorado is a proud member of
the Association of American University Presses.

The University Press of Colorado is a cooperative publishing enterprise supported, in part,
by Adams State University, Colorado State University, Fort Lewis College, Metropolitan
State University of Denver, Regis University, University of Colorado, University of Northern
Colorado, Utah State University, and Western State Colorado University.

∞ This paper meets the requirements of the ANSI/NISO Z39.48-1992 (Permanence of Paper).

"Dominguez," "Nihongo Gakko," and "Swimming in the American" were previously published
in Hiroshi Kashiwagi's *Swimming in the American: A Memoir and Selected Writings* (San Mateo,
CA: Asian American Curriculum Project, 2005).

Library of Congress Cataloging-in-Publication Data

Kashiwagi, Hiroshi, 1922–
  Starting from Loomis and other stories / Hiroshi Kashiwagi ; edited with an introduction by
Tim Yamamura ; afterword by Lane Ryo Hirabayashi.
    pages cm. — (George and Sakaye Aratani Nikkei in the Americas series)
  ISBN 978-1-60732-253-5 (pbk.) — ISBN 978-1-60732-254-2 (ebook)
  1. Kashiwagi, Hiroshi, 1922– 2. Japanese Americans—California—Biography. 3. California—
Biography. I. Yamamura, Tim. II. Title.
  F870.J3K259 2013
  973'.04956—dc23
                    2013024667

Design by Daniel Pratt

22 21 20 19 18 17 16 15 14 13   10 9 8 7 6 5 4 3 2 1

Cover photograph by E. N. Matsuba

To my wife, Sadako,

and in memory of
Dr. James Akira Hirabayashi

Contents

∽∾∽

Figures

❦

FIGURES

———

Acknowledgments

For making this publication possible, I wish to thank Professor Lane Ryo Hirabayashi, UCLA, general editor, George and Sakaye Aratani Nikkei in the Americas Series; the editorial board and staff of the University Press of Colorado; editor Tim Yamamura for his invaluable assistance; and my wife, Sadako, for her constant love and support.

I would also like to remember my parents—my father, Fukumatsu, from whom I received the literary bent, and my mother, Kofusa, who left us gold coins, so precious today.

Starting from Loomis

Hiroshi Kashiwagi: A Disquieted American

Tim Yamamura

For over eighty years, Hiroshi Kashiwagi has been quietly building an eclectic and accomplished career in the arts as a playwright, poet, performer, and librarian. As a Nisei (first generation born of immigrant parents), Kashiwagi has lived through the major eras in Japanese American history, most notably the community's wartime incarceration after the Japanese attack on Pearl Harbor. Because of the choices he made as a young man while confined at Tule Lake in resistance to the government's infamous loyalty questionnaire,[1] Kashiwagi has carried a stigma for the remainder of his life, one that has hung over him like a dark cloud: "No-No Boy."

As a Nisei writer, his work belongs on the shelf with notables like John Okada, Hisaye Yamamoto, Wakako Yamauchi, Yoshiko Uchida, and Toshio Mori—the foundation of Japanese American writing. He has been celebrated for his courage to "write beyond the stereotype of the Japanese American internee as helpless, innocent victim and to explore the dark side of Japanese America" (Chan et al. 1991, 314). As a playwright and actor, he was influential in the origins of Japanese American and Asian American theater, performing with fellow community members in the Tule Lake Little Theater, in groups he helped found (like the postwar Nisei Experimental Group), and in early

Asian American Theater Company productions. Commenting on his influence, the acclaimed playwright Philip Kan Gotanda called Kashiwagi "seminal to the whole lineage of Japanese American playwrights" (quoted in Nakao 2005). Furthermore, as a living testament to the injustices 120,000 people of Japanese ancestry faced during the war, he has been called upon by generations after him to bear witness to the past, to speak out and educate others on the importance of civil liberties and on lessons to be learned from elders, all the while trusting his story to those who "seek the history / from those of us who lived it" (Kashiwagi 2005, 171).

Beyond his significance to younger artists, activists, and community members who have looked to him for a sense of legacy, Kashiwagi's expression has also been driven by something deeply personal: a struggle to live and write on his own terms in light of his disquieting past. Since the war years, the writer and performer has pursued numerous projects—including his play, *The Betrayed* (1993); his autobiographical, multi-generic work *Swimming in the American* (2005); and his recent collection of poetry, *Ocean Beach* (2010)—each largely committed to examining the difficult conditions and painful choices imposed upon him, his family, and his fellow Japanese Americans by the US government during and after the Pacific War. Well over half a century after the war, even though Kashiwagi never "fought," his writings can still be read as a search for a sense of peace, one history has denied him.

This book, *Starting from Loomis and Other Stories*, is his latest project. It is a memoir, a cycle of stories that present a dynamic portrait of an aging man trying to remember himself as a younger man. It is the product of numerous writings Kashiwagi has done over the years, a partnership with the University Press of Colorado and Professor Lane Hirabayashi (the George and Sakaye Aratani Nikkei in the Americas series editor), as well as a year of experimentation, rewriting, and honest dialogue between me and the author. As the book's editor, I can say that the process has been a pleasure, a distinct honor, and a rare learning experience. In the pieces that follow—all based on something related to the author's life—Kashiwagi recalls and reflects upon the moments, people, forces, mysteries, and choices that have made him the man he is. This book is about the things in Kashiwagi's life he can't forget.

We begin where Kashiwagi himself began, in Loomis, California, a small town near Sacramento, in the 1920s and 1930s. The reader learns of Kashiwagi's early years, his challenges with learning English and relating to the world outside his home, and the socioeconomic conditions under which he and his immigrant family struggled. We gain insight into the defining role family played in the decisions Kashiwagi made in the early decades of his life—particularly in the years leading up to and during World War II. Finally, simmering in the opening pages is a central theme of *Starting from Loomis* as well as his entire oeuvre, one the author returns to again and again in the book: the discrepant struggles of ethnic minorities in an American society plagued by racism, exploitation, and class subordination. The first set of vignettes and reflections introduces the historical threads to be followed throughout the book, all of which began in Loomis, where he grew up. This is the America in which the young Kashiwagi grew up, one an older Kashiwagi cannot help but remember. Kashiwagi brings the title story to a close by introducing his experiences while held prisoner at what is arguably America's most infamous wartime concentration camp: Tule Lake. This includes decisions that have haunted him for the rest of his life, all stemming from the registration and subsequent loyalty questionnaire that he, with his family, chose to resist.

Although the stories collected here explore the author's experiences from childhood on, the book differs from a conventional autobiography. This is not a simple bildungsroman, or "coming of age" narrative; nor do the stories follow a neat linear logic or depict a singular journey of self-realization. What distinguishes Kashiwagi's project in terms of content and form is both the positionality from which he writes and the manner in which he chooses to present his story. Just as Kashiwagi remembers and re-presents his world beginning in Loomis, his stories also reveal the life of an older man determined to look back, to return to his past to ask himself "Why? Why did this happen? What does it mean? What is my story?" The pieces capture a mind compelled to return to moments and sites significant to the author's life, a conscience driven to understand, explain, often laugh about, but also to rework his place within the history he lived. Although the book does possess a timeline—his early years in the Loomis community until his father departed for a sanatorium in Part I and to Tule Lake and the years after in Part II—the collection can also be read as a churning assemblage of remembrances, poetic musings, (re-)imaginings, demonstrations, tangents, tall tales, and investigations. The fragmentary, nonlinear, multi-generic format of his writing, I would argue, not only reflects the fragmentations of memory induced by such traumas as racism, forced removal, and incarceration but can also be read as a bold personal response to the impossible conditions he and other Nisei faced after Pearl Harbor—demonized by the American government, press, and public; denied their civil rights; but nonetheless compelled by their government to declare their loyalties to a country that, in Kashiwagi's words, was not able to be "fair and trusting" in the treatment of its citizens (Kashiwagi 2005, 91).

Kashiwagi was probably like other Japanese Americans in ultimately placing the welfare of his family over the dictates of national belonging. His work at times is also reminiscent of other Nisei writers, such as Toshio Mori, Hisaye Yamamoto, and Wakako Yamauchi, who wrote zuihitsu-like (miscellany) short pieces consisting of personal reflections and vignettes on the happenings of everyday life as well as major historical events. Yet his narrative is unique in that it is one of the few memoirs or even recorded testimonies to capture the experiences of a Japanese American who would become a No-No Boy and would thus carry the stain of one deemed disloyal long after the war; in this respect, his work helps clarify if not a mode of Japanese American writing, at least a particular predicament all Nisei writers who survived the camps—albeit in their respective ways—have had to contend with in the years since. For Kashiwagi, as a racialized, minoritized writer and one who endured unjust incarceration because of his Japanese ancestry, the act of remembrance in writing is always marked by the cloud of suspicion that hung over his generation after Pearl Harbor. His narrative and autobiographical mode not only enacts the traumas of his past but therein confronts a question that haunts the genre of memoir: the question of authorial reliability. How can Hiroshi Kashiwagi tell the truth of his life in a country that did not trust him?

The pages that follow offer an answer to that question. The author does not pretend to remember everything about the past; nor does Kashiwagi claim to speak for all Japanese Americans (although he does claim his place as a major voice within the archive of his generation, the Nisei, from which he has felt alienated by the label No-No Boy). Furthermore, as with all narratives born from memory, the life this book portrays lies in both the author's silences and his revelations. What Kashiwagi *can* do is grapple with his past—the history he lived and the mysteries of memory itself—with honesty, humor, and a rare clarity of purpose. What he offers is a narrative crafted with conscience and care, one informed by a sense of justice and a fidelity to the past. It is the portrait of a lifetime spent confronting the unforgettable.

As readers engage with Kashiwagi's stories, as we learn of his triumphs and trials, as we struggle with him through the choices he made and the times in which he lived, the book makes clear the cost of discrimination and scapegoating, as well as the limitations of militarized "yes/no, with-us-or-against-us" thinking—both then and now, in times of war and in war's wake. In an era filled with the language of terror, Islamophobia, racialized antagonisms, and immigrant scapegoating, Kashiwagi's voice speaks to the irreducibility of life to readymade judgments or uncritical labeling, regardless of which side of whatever fence we seem to fall at a given time. He asks us to contend with the historical forces underwriting our lives and, in that light, to measure the quality of conscience we bring to our determinations.

Note

1. In January 1943 the US Department of War issued a loyalty questionnaire entitled "Statement of United States Citizenship of Japanese Ancestry." Intended to ascertain the "allegiances" of those in camp, the key questions referenced in Kashiwagi's story are numbers 27 and 28, which read: "no. 27. Are you willing to serve in the armed forces of the United States on combat duty wherever ordered; and no. 28. Will you swear unqualified allegiance to the United States of America and faithfully defend the United States from any or all attack by foreign or domestic forces, and forswear any form of allegiance or obedience to the Japanese emperor, or any other foreign government, power or organization?"

References

Chan, Jeffery Paul, Frank Chin, Lawson Fusao Inada, and Shawn Wong. 1991. *The Big Aiiieeeee! An Anthology of Chinese American and Japanese American Literature*. New York: Meridian.

Kashiwagi, Hiroshi. 2005. *Swimming in the American: A Memoir and Selected Writings*. San Mateo, CA: Asian American Curriculum Project.

Nakao, Annie. 2005. "Pioneering Poet, Playwright, and Actor Focuses on His Life in His First Book—at Age 82." *San Francisco Chronicle*, April 26.

PART I

Starting from Loomis

❧

There were over 150 Japanese families living in Loomis. It was a large community for such a small town. In the schools, too, there were a lot of Japanese kids. I started school in 1928; we were living in the country, so I rode the bus the school provided. I spoke only Japanese then; what little English I knew I picked up during the few miserable months I spent in kindergarten.

Reading was daunting. Father helped me every night through the first two readers, laboriously sounding out the words in a heavy accent. With the third reader he threw up his hands and told me I was on my own.

I believe we Japanese children were segregated or tracked at public school. We were so happy in our school that I didn't realize we had this odd arrangement until recently. From the fifth through eighth grades I had the same teacher and the same classmates, plus or minus a few. "Mrs. Land was promoted too," we said of our teacher, who followed us every year. In our grade there were two sections—one made up of Caucasian children of ranch owners, storekeepers, officials, and other prominent persons and a sprinkling of Japanese. I don't know how the Japanese were chosen for that class; I suppose they were considered better students, though some of us in the other class made higher scores on tests.

DOI: 10.5876/9781607322542.c01

———

Our section consisted of Japanese, Portuguese, Spanish, and poor white kids, some of whom came to school barefoot. It was during the Depression, though we Japanese always wore clean and decent clothes—which meant no patches. Once after school, when I was home and had changed my clothes, I had on a pair of overalls with patches on my seat. A boy who was at our house called me "patch-ass." I remember how hurtful and humiliating that was.

I guess we were the "B" class. Mrs. Land, bless her, kept harping on our grammar and "pidgin English," so much so that we all learned to speak correctly, at least in her presence. Some of those who were picked on a lot said Mrs. Land didn't like Japanese. I don't think that was the case; I thought she was a good teacher, really concerned for us.

I wasn't called on much, which was lucky because I didn't always know the answers—I just pretended that I did. Even so, on my report card Mrs. Land wrote tersely, "he is intelligent and sensitive."

Most of the Japanese who lived in Loomis were farmers. A few owned their farms; they had bought them before the 1913 Alien Land Law was enacted, which forbade the ownership of land by Issei (first-generation Japanese). After 1913, some bought land in the name of their citizen children to get around this law. But most Japanese leased the farms or sharecropped.

From the time I was a child, around ten or eleven, I was out in the orchard picking fruit—plums, peaches, and pears—in the summer. I remember when I first started I was paid fifty cents a day. It was kid's pay, though I think I was doing an adult's work.

When I was paid at the end of the summer, I was called to Mr. Okusu's office, which consisted of a simple rolltop desk with piles of papers and accounting books and a chair in the corner of the parlor. As he handed me the check he said, "You worked hard for this, now spend it wisely," and I said, "*Hai* [yes], thank you," with, of course, a bow. I don't remember the amount of the check, but to me it seemed a princely sum. In fact, I had never had a check in my name, much less for such an amount.

We got along with the Caucasian kids at school and in the neighborhood as long as we remembered our place. We were the Japanese kids whose parents worked the farms, who lived in shacks, took *furo* (Japanese baths), and only wore *zori* (flip-flops) inside the house and to and from the bathhouse; we ate fish, rice, tofu, sushi, and other weird things.

I had a few white friends, but we were never very close. I don't remember ever going inside a *hakujin* (Caucasian) home, and I don't remember them coming to our house. When we had the store in town, a few came to shop, especially in the late spring or summer when Mama sold snow cones. I wonder if it was in response to the ad a fellow student (I think a girl from the eighth grade) had solicited and put in the school newsletter—"Get Mama's Snowcones at Loomis Fish Market." That was definitely a good time for the store and a busy time for Mother.

In 1941, the family was sharecropping a ranch in Penryn, a small but active town about three miles from Loomis. Father had already gone to the sanatorium because of his tuberculosis, so Mother was the head of the household and had to make the difficult decisions. Mother was around thirty-eight at the time; I know she wasn't quite forty. The running joke later was that she was never forty, always claiming to be thirty-nine (she was like Jack Benny in that respect).

I had recently returned from Los Angeles. My parents were fearful that I would catch my father's TB since I had lung issues as a child, so they sent me to Los Angeles to finish my last year of high school. I was back with my family again and, along with my mother and younger brother and sister, doing all I could to help the family make ends meet.

The small twenty-acre ranch where we lived was our main source of income. We were allowed a monthly advance of fifty dollars on the crop to live on. This was hardly enough, and we had to supplement it with our savings or what we earned working at other ranches in the summer. After our harvest in late August, we went to pick grapes in Lodi, a town about forty miles away, living in a labor camp for two months. We would come home with a tidy sum that would see us through the winter months.

We had a flock of New Hampshire chickens we had raised from day-old chicks. The roosters were butchered on special occasions, and the hens provided a plentiful supply of eggs; the surplus we bartered for groceries. Mother's vegetable garden was a source of fresh vegetables throughout the year.

Togan (Chinese winter melon) grew abundantly. The greenish gray melons looked like huge stones in the garden. Togan soup was our comfort food. I suppose it was a Japanese version of a Chinese dish. I make it now, trying to duplicate Mother's soup—the distinctive taste and smell of togan mixed with pork, dried shrimp, and shiitake mushrooms. I love it. It takes me back to those early days when my mother, like other resourceful Issei mothers, accomplished so much with so little. Togan soup—so warming and filling and good. I remember how happy it made me; I would have it every day if my wife would allow it.

After the fruit harvest, after all the expenses had been deducted, we shared the net income 60/40—60 percent for the owner and 40 percent for us, less the advance we had already spent during the year. Some years we made a few hundred dollars, but I don't remember ever making over $500.

At the time of the evacuation order, Executive Order 9066, we had been working since the end of the previous season, and we left for camp in May 1942, which was before the harvest. This meant that, except for the monthly advances, we were not fully compensated for the days we had worked—Mother, my brother, and I, who worked after school and on weekends.

When we were about to leave for camp, the boss asked us, "Are you okay? Is it okay?" He probably would have given us some of our wages if we had asked, but we didn't know at the time that it was within our right, so we told him we would be okay—we lost most of our season's wages that year. He did give us fifty dollars for leaving our pickup truck with him. He was a kind man, thoughtful and sweet. He used to bring us the *Sacramento Bee* every night after he and his family were through with it.

We said goodbye to the boss and transported ourselves on the pickup to Loomis, three miles away. The fruit house was the gathering place from where we boarded a bus to Arboga Assembly Center near Marysville, about ten miles away. After unloading our suitcases and duffle bags I drove the pickup to the Ford garage in town, where I left it for the boss by previous arrangement. Then I went to join my family and face the unknown future of life in camp.

I once wrote a poem that stated that on December 7, 1941, when I heard the radio report that Japan had attacked Pearl Harbor, I, a Japanese American, was chopping wood left-handed. I'm not sure what I was trying to say. It's true that I'm a natural-born "lefty," partly converted by my parents to be a "righty," as was customary at the time. To this day I often feel an ache, a frustration, in one hand over the other, as if one side of me is always neglected or ignored while the other is in use.

Perhaps in the poem I was trying to relate this feeling to my reaction to the devastating news. Of course, my first reaction was shock and disbelief. Soon after, though, I wondered what would happen to us Japanese Americans. Who are we? How are we perceived by others? What will happen now that war has begun?

My younger brother and sister were attending Placer Union High School, riding the school bus from Penryn to Auburn, a distance of seven miles. Though the situation was awkward, they didn't report anything unpleasant happening after Pearl Harbor. Most of the teachers were fair, telling the students that we were Americans like everyone else.

However, some teachers could barely contain their hate and prejudice, including my public speaking teacher who I thought had been my favorite. I understand that as soon as the Japanese were gone, she was active in a committee to keep the "Japs" from returning to Auburn. When I was in Arboga, I remember writing to her for advice on forming a drama club, and I never heard from her. I was certainly wrong about her.

The *Nichi Bei* newspaper was our primary and most reliable source of information. *Nichi Bei* provided an invaluable service to our community during those trying days until the very last day it was permitted to publish. Other metropolitan papers and radio stations were unreliable, filled with sensational and alarming reports—war hysteria was in the air.

As we prepared to leave for camp, Mother made two rather large duffle bags, sewing them by hand because the canvas material was too thick for her treadle sewing machine. The material was cut from the tent my father had put up when he tried to isolate himself in the pasture because of his TB. It was amazing how much those bags could hold. We were able to take far more than what would fit in an average suitcase. I still have one of the bags somewhere. It's a reminder not only of how resourceful Mother was but also of all Father was willing to sacrifice for us.

—⁓⁓—

We first went by bus to Arboga Assembly Center. Barracks had been hastily built on what had been a pasture—swampland—which had been leveled by a bulldozer. The mosquitoes and gnats were vicious, especially with the women, feeding on their exposed arms and legs. I think this was when they took to wearing slacks—not as a fashion statement but as a survival mechanism.

Our quarters in the tarpapered barrack consisted of a single room with four US Army cots, mattresses, and blankets. The partitions on both sides of the room did not go to the top, so we could hear everything going on in the rest of the barrack. Of course, whatever we said or did could also be heard by the others. But I found the cot fairly comfortable and slept well enough at night.

For our meals, we lined up with our tin plates. God, how I hate food heaped on tin plates and those tables with built-in benches. Even now at picnics I dislike those tables. The food, though plentiful, was poorly prepared by well-intentioned but amateur cooks. Despite their white aprons and chef's hats, they fooled no one; they were still former farmers, students, insurance agents, fruit pickers, fishermen, and janitors—hardly cooks.

Camp was a great equalizer. Everyone, no matter what his or her background or previous position in society, was reduced to a number. It was possible to go to the shower room and run into the former president of the Japanese Association or the priest from the temple or Mr. Sasaki, the boss and owner of a sixty-acre ranch who always wore a straw hat on a summer Sunday. Without their clothes on, it was almost possible not to recognize them. In fact, that is what we all sought, anonymity, especially in the shower room.

What was most outrageous was going to the latrine, a public outhouse with accommodations for eight or so without partitions. We sat there cheek-to-cheek, so to speak. An often-heard remark was *erai toko de aimasu, nah*. I don't know how to translate this properly; perhaps "what a horrible place to meet" or "what a miserable situation" . . . something like that.

I was quite active at Arboga. I had been out of high school for almost two years, anxiously waiting for my brother to graduate so I could go on to college. He was to have graduated in June, but he didn't quite make it as we were ordered to go in May. Freed from the drudgery of farmwork, I found life in Arboga fascinating and challenging; there were so many new people.

I threw myself into the various activities of camp life. I attended meetings of every kind, participated actively, and volunteered for almost everything. Soon I was working as an orderly at the hospital and writing for the camp newspaper, pursuing areas of interest to me. Most Nisei with any ambition hoped to become medical doctors who would serve their own people, and I was no exception; that seemed to be the only profession open to Japanese Americans. I also liked to write, even though I knew it was an impractical pursuit. I think my father was rather pleased with my writing interest as he was an inveterate letter writer and reader himself.

Letter writing was the only contact we would have with Father from that point on. We spent May to August 1942 at Arboga. Even though it meant packing and moving again, we were glad when the order came to transfer to a more permanent camp at Tule Lake.

On the train trip to Tule Lake I was assigned to be monitor of our car, responsible for about thirty passengers, as a result of my active life at Arboga. It was an easy assignment; the shades were drawn, our movements were restricted, and there was very little interaction among the people. They sat quietly, grimly, preoccupied with their thoughts, trying to endure the discomfort of the ancient train—the cobwebs overhead and the hard wooden benches. It was a long trip, a long night, and none of us slept much. At the designated time I distributed sandwiches and milk to the people, some of whom weren't interested in eating. There was baby food for mothers with infants.

When we arrived at Tule Lake in the morning, we were welcomed by a man who claimed to be our block manager. Though he was a stranger who we later thought was a bit officious, it was nice to have someone greet us when we arrived at this desolate, strange place near the northern border of California. "If you need anything, just ask me," he said. He provided us with mattresses and US Army blankets; we unpacked and settled in.

After the miserable experience in Arboga, we were excited about the flush toilets in the latrines; in fact, we made a special trip to the latrine to check them out—two rows of porcelain toilets that actually flushed. We tried them several times to see if they really worked; they did. However, the lack of partitions between the toilets and the trough urinals was disconcerting.

One of the first things I did was look for work. I took the most available job as a carpenter's helper, putting up sheetrock in the apartments. I joined a motley crew of five or six men of disparate ages. I believe I was the youngest among them. Except for the crew chief, none of us had any experience in carpentry, barely able to hit a nail straight, but we were welcomed everywhere as *daiku-san* (carpenters). People moved out all their furniture—cots, crude tables and chairs, hastily made from scrap lumber—and waited for us. We were served sodas and refreshments and treated rather royally, which to me was embarrassing as I thought we didn't deserve it. We were just doing a job, making the quarters more livable, finishing what the government had failed to do.

A typical day in camp would begin with the mess bell for breakfast. Getting up was routine, but breakfast, which was usually hotcakes— not my favorite, especially when they were served cold on metal platters—was not much of an inducement. I had never liked the alternative, cereals, dry or cooked, so I often skipped breakfast.

I had worked as a "schoolboy," or houseboy, in Los Angeles and acquired a taste for lamb and mutton, which was fortunate as lamb or mutton stew was a dish Nihonjin (Japanese) usually disliked. They served a lot of it in the camps. So there would often be an entire platter of the stew that I could enjoy to my heart's content at dinnertime.

My mother had sold fish at the store in Loomis, and our friend had worked for many years at the Capital Fish Company in Sacramento and had contacts with wholesalers outside. Both knew their fish well; they also knew how much Japanese loved fish, how they craved fresh fish, which was rarely served in the mess hall.

They decided to use what savings they had to start a cottage business selling fresh fish. They put in an order with Paladini Fish Company in San Francisco, and within a week a box of fish packed in ice arrived by railway express and was delivered to our door. We would leave the box outside on the shady side of the barrack, and the fish would stay fresh for several days. No matter how hot it got during the day, it was always cool or even cold in the shade.

What was fun was watching people who came from blocks around— seeing their expressions of pleasure ogling the fish, then buying some, knowing full well it was a luxury since meals were provided in the mess hall. Within a day or two most of the fish were sold; those that were left, usually smaller fish like mackerel, kingfish, or sardine, were salted lightly and left out in the sun to dry. After trying the dried kingfish, quickly cooked on a potbellied stove, I realized why it was so highly sought after—it was incredibly good. Mother and our friend sold a lot of fish and built a modest nest egg during that time.

I belonged to the Tule Lake Writers Club and the Tule Lake Little Theater, administered by the camp recreation department. Both were great creative outlets for me, and they gave me a chance to pursue my interest in the arts. Strangely, going to camp was an exciting time for me; I was able to do what I absolutely loved to do . . . at least at first.

The writers club met once a week. When I was involved in a play, I was at the theater every night, either rehearsing or performing.

Everyone in the writers club was encouraged to write something to be read to the group for comments and criticisms. Not everyone wrote; I learned later that many were there as observers.

Those who wrote were writing about life before camp—about city life and college life, both new and unfamiliar to me. Some wrote fiction in the hard-boiled detective mode or in the Dos Passos or Hemingway style. It all sounded great and everyone was impressed, including me.

Most of the members were college students from the University of California (UC) at Berkeley or UCLA; to me, a mere high school graduate and a country kid at that, they seemed highly educated and very sophisticated. I knew I didn't belong with them, but my interest in writing drew me to the club. Feeling small and inadequate, I sat quietly, watching and listening to what went on.

I wrote a story based on something that happened just before evacuation; it was autobiographical, handwritten, about a country boy longing for a radio and finally one day going by Greyhound bus to Sacramento where he bought a small Zenith radio. What a thrill that was—a brand-new radio, all his own, that played loudly and clearly, especially at night. But he didn't get to enjoy it for long because of the war and evacuation.

I don't remember what happened after that. I remember that the story was titled "The Zenith Radio." After I finished reading it to the group, I thought there would be some reaction but there was none, just silence. Why didn't they say something? Did they not like it? I have often wondered. Or did they resent the fact that this young country hick had shown them up, had written a story that had moved them; or was the story too close to home?

Based on their silence, I decided it wasn't much of a story. Later, the leader of the club wanted to publish the story and asked me for it, but I had thrown it out. I realize now that I missed a rare opportunity as the magazine *Tulean Interlude*, a collection of writings done in camp, became a primary source material for scholars and is deposited in the Bancroft Library at UC Berkeley, along with other camp documents.

These are among the memories that have stayed with me through the years. But like everything else in camp, these pursuits were only a temporary diversion from the harsh realities imposed upon us by the war.

In January 1943 the US Department of War issued a loyalty questionnaire entitled "Statement of United States Citizenship of Japanese Ancestry." The key questions were numbers 27 and 28, which read:

> No. 27. Are you willing to serve in the armed forces of the United States on combat duty wherever ordered?

> No. 28. Will you swear unqualified allegiance to the United States of America and faithfully defend the United States from any or all attack by foreign or domestic forces, and forswear any form of allegiance or obedience to the Japanese emperor, or any other foreign government, power or organization?

The War Relocation Authority (WRA) used the same questionnaire to identify Japanese Americans who could be released from camp.

The process was called "Registration." Right away, our family was caught up in the confusion over the loyalty questions and went to see what the others were doing. In our family, the burden fell heavily on my mother. Her primary concern was to keep us together; her fear was that if we registered, my brother and I would be forced out of camp, possibly into the service, and the family would be broken up further. If my father had been with us, I don't know what we would have done, what his decision would have been. I know it would have been much easier for us because he would have made the decision and we would have either followed it or not.

Here was my position: why was I, an American citizen, thrown in prison without cause, without due process? I had registered for the draft, as required of citizens of my age and sex in 1942; why were they questioning my loyalty now? How could they do that? I was an American, a loyal American. If they restored my status as a rightful citizen, let me go free, out of this prison, I would do anything required of me. Why should I answer the questions? I would follow my conscience and refuse to register.

Block 42 was one of the first ordered to register. Most of the young men there had signed up for "repatriation" to Japan, an ironic choice since they were all citizens of the United States and many had never been to Japan. I think the administration picked them first to register as punishment.

When no one appeared at the block office on the designated day, the authorities took action. Around five o'clock in the afternoon the mess bells rang out, urgently and alarmingly, announcing the arrival of soldiers to round up the recalcitrant young men. The young men were forced onto the army truck at bayonet point. Everyone was outraged, and emotions ran high. Mothers, girlfriends, brothers, and sisters tearfully bid goodbye to the young men who were being taken to the county jail outside of camp. This show of force by the administration was meant to break down our resistance, but it only hardened our resolve to resist. We returned to our apartment to pack our bags and await our turn to be taken.

But the Block 42 men were soon released because the WRA had no cause to hold them. We continued to resist, and nothing happened. Years later, I was devastated to read in Michi Weglyn's classic *Years of Infamy* that the registration order had not been compulsory; there was nothing compelling us to register other than their threats, a fact the administration never disclosed to us. To this day, many believe the order was compulsory.

Furthermore, the threat of twenty years in jail and/or a $10,000 fine for noncompliance had been just that: a threat, all lies. Laboring under these conditions, fearful and uncertain, everyone at Tule Lake had to make their choice: either we answered yes or no, or we refused to answer the loyalty questions.

Since we refused to register, my family and I were called before camp officials to clarify our position regarding the questionnaire in August of the same year, six months after registration. I told the official that I did not want to answer the questions while I was held in camp and treated as if I were a dangerous alien. I said it was unfair to ask this only of American Japanese and not of American Germans and American Italians. I tried to make my case, but the official said I had no choice—I had to answer the questions one way or another. I gave "no" answers in protest of what my government had done to me and my family.

For following our conscience, we were held back at Tule Lake while those who professed their loyalty by answering yes/yes to the questions were allowed to leave camp. The majority went to the East Coast.

Tule Lake became a segregation center, a maximum security prison for "disloyal" Americans. And we became known as the infamous "No-No Boys," a stigma that would mark us whenever the subject of camps came up, which was often.

Among Japanese Americans, the most common question upon meeting after the war was, what camp were you in? Since camp was our shared experience, I suppose the question is a natural lead-in to a conversation, but I dreaded it. I hated to lie so I always answered directly, "I was at Tule Lake." Think whatever you want; I did what I had to do. I'm not proud of it and I'm not ashamed of it . . . or am I? Or are you making me feel ashamed?

Because of this difficulty, I felt alienated from the community and tried to avoid other Japanese as much as possible after the war. In college, I acquired a reputation for being eccentric or even arrogant for refusing to socialize with other Japanese American students. Most of my college friends were actually white veterans who were not interested in wartime experiences, theirs or anyone else's. Their goal was to complete their education under the GI Bill.

The camps we went to were officially called Arboga Assembly Center and Tule Lake Relocation Center. No matter what the government insisted on calling them—internment camps, relocation centers, or any other name—they were still prisons. There was barbed-wire fence with guard towers manned by MPs armed with rifles and machine guns directed toward us—the inmates.

The searchlights from the guard towers were eerie at night. Many of the soldiers were recent transfers from the war in the South Pacific, young, nervous, and trigger-happy. We didn't dare go near the fence for fear of being shot at—there were tragic instances of that. But aside from the physical confinement was the invisible fence enclosing our spirit; this imprisonment of the spirit, the psychological effect, even more than the actual fence, was the most ravaging part of the camp experience, leaving a scar that would remain with us for the rest of our lives. I can certainly attest to that.

My Parents

Rarely does a day go by when my thoughts don't turn to my parents, Fukumatsu and Kofusa, an unlikely couple who first met at Angel Island—she a seventeen-year-old picture bride, he a man of the world, age thirty-one. Both were attractive people, and I often wonder if that was the reason for their tempestuous life together. No, I don't think it was vanity; it was more their character. They were fairly similar— strong-willed and unbending. When he tried to dominate her, there was tension because she would not relent, always standing her ground, asserting her place. They fought a lot, causing much grief for us children. We looked for the times when they were loving. Those moments were so beautiful.

Sometimes after our bath, when we were sitting around the kitchen table, Father would say, "How about making some *dango*, Mama? "Isn't it late, Papa?" Mother would say; but I knew we would have dango— our version of a pancake—one huge cake as big as the large frying pan in which it was cooked. Mother would fire up the Wedgewood stove and quickly prepare the batter, and soon we would have our dango.

DOI: 10.5876/9781607322542:c02

Then each of the four of us—my father, brother, sister, and I—would break off a piece and eat it with melting butter and blackberry jam.

"This is good," Father would say, and we would all agree. "Have some too, Mama?"

"It is so late," Mother would say, but she would join us and Father would laugh.

We always ate it with our hands, the real butter melting from the heat of the dango and the sweet-tart blackberry jam. Today I insist on maple syrup with my pancakes, but the blackberry jam was special, made with blackberries that grew wild in the country. The dango scene is a happy memory. The dango tasted like nothing I've had since.

I think they stayed together because of us—the children—and because of the hostile environment outside the home. But their life together was quite brief—just twenty years. Fukumatsu developed tuberculosis and lived in isolation from his family and friends until his death, first in a tent he set up in a field behind our house and then in a sanatorium before and during the war. When he died years later, emphysema was given as the official cause of death, but his lungs had been ravaged by so many years of disease. Kofusa died at age eighty-two, spending the latter half of her life free and independent, something she had always fought for. But it was a widow's life, lonely and incomplete.

As long as the blood coursing through me is warm, Fukumatsu and Kofusa will be with me. I embody them both, the good and the bad, the sad and the happy.

Sacramento Nihonmachi

This journey to early Sacramento Nihonmachi begins at the Southern Pacific station on I Street, a short distance from the boardinghouse where we stayed on occasion during the time we lived in Loomis. Actually, I don't remember ever going inside the station. It was rather forbidding, enclosed within an iron fence and gate. But I was always conscious of the trains coming and going, day and night, whenever we were at the boardinghouse, Nankai-ya.

A haven for folks from Wakayama Prefecture in Japan, Nankai-ya was run by a family from Wakayama who were related to my father. We were always put up in a room by the front window on the second floor. This was a choice room reserved for relatives, but it was no different from the other rooms for families and permanent guests. Bachelors and migrant workers who stayed between harvests and in the winter were housed in the basement.

I have three vivid memories from the boardinghouse. First was the horse-drawn ice cream carriage that came several times a day. I don't remember the ice cream so much (we were rarely treated to it), but I can still hear the tinkling bells—so distinctive and tantalizing.

DOI: 10.5876/9781607322542.c03

Next was my first taste of peanut butter. One morning the board-inghouse manager held up a paper carton box and announced that he had a wonderful new product called "pea-nuts buttah." He spooned a generous portion and told me to taste it, which I did. I thought it tasted rather odd but nodded my approval.

Then there was the chow mein. There were many Chinese fam-ilies living on I Street and many businesses, mostly underground. Sometimes we'd place an order for chow mein from one of the restau-rants. Soon a Chinese waiter would march in, holding a platter of chow mein high above his shoulder. I don't remember the taste of the chow mein, but I never forgot the theatrical waiter and the delicious aroma of the I Street chow mein—that was magical for me.

I Street seemed a world away from Nihonmachi, which was centered down the street on L Street between 3rd and 4th Streets. Loomis is about twenty-five miles east of Sacramento Nihonmachi. My parents ran a fish market/grocery store, and Father made weekly buying trips to Sacramento. Sometimes in the summer when school was out, I got to go with him.

Father tended to favor places run by fellow Wakayama folks, such as Sakiyama Dry Goods Store, which was on the corner of 3rd and M Streets. That's where he bought a pair of heavy coats for my brother and me. Those coats were the bane of our childhood. I suppose they were good coats—imitation leather, which was impervious to rain and lined with warm sheepskin. The problem was that when it got hot, the coats tended to smell like sheep, no, more like sheep urine. The real problem was that no one else in school had such a coat. We tried to lose them, but someone would always find them and return them to us. And they were absolutely indestructible! The only solution was to outgrow them, which we finally did after many agonizing years.

My father used to buy gift items at Yorozu-ya on the corner of 4th and M Streets. My memory of that store is that Mr. Okada, the proprietor and an elder of the *kendo* (fencing) group, once presented me with a prize for winning a few matches at the kendo tournament held at the Buddhist Hall on O Street. The prize, nicely boxed and wrapped, was a *tenugui*, or towel. What was special was that my name appeared in the Japanese section of a community newspaper for the first time.

Whenever we went to Sacramento as a family, it was our custom to have noodles at this hole-in-the-wall noodle shop. I think it was off of an alley. There were five of us, but we always ordered six bowls of tempura noodles, and the befuddled waitress would look for the extra person in our party. Of course, there was no such person; the extra bowl was for my mother, who always had two bowls. This remained a standing joke in the family until late in her life, when she lost all interest in noodles.

Our favorite place was the New Eagle Drug Store on the corner of 4th and O Streets, next to Agnes Hospital. I think my father stopped there whenever he was in Sacramento. Besides medicine and sundries, he got his monthly magazines there, such as *King* and *Shufu no Tomo* (*Housewives' Companion*) for Mother. He also went there for advice and general information. Ishii-san, the pharmacist and owner, was knowledgeable on just about any subject and most accommodating to his customers and friends. It was he who recommended the Caucasian doctor who operated on me when I had blood poisoning and spent a week at Agnes Hospital.

The hospital, owned by the Miyakawa family, was named after Agnes Miyakawa, who became a noted opera singer. I learned recently that the nurses were all Caucasian. I believe they were, but I remember one Japanese nurse who used to give me candy for "being such a good boy." A few years ago I met one of the sons of the Miyakawa family and told him the story of my surgery. As a child, I explained, I once had blood poisoning and had to be operated on at the hospital. He did not believe me, so I showed him the scar on my neck to convince him. The proof was in the scars still on my skin.

Sacramento Nihonmachi has always been a magical place for me—so different from bucolic Loomis where I grew up.

Nihongo Gakko

JAPANESE-LANGUAGE SCHOOL

The last time I met my friend Jack in Loomis, he reminded me of a bit of history we share. "We go back a long way, don't we? We used to go to Japanese school together," he said, and I was reminded of the carpool our families used to have when we were kids. Every Saturday morning his father, with Jack and his brother in tow, would stop for me on the way to Nihongo Gakko in Penryn. This was convenient, but it meant I had to be up and ready and not pretend to be sick. My father would be busy with his work as a fish peddler, but by four in the afternoon, when school let out, he would be there to drive us home.

"Sometimes your father didn't show up and we had to walk," Jack said. I didn't think that happened too often. Of course, I only had to walk three miles back to Loomis town, while Jack and his brother had three or four more miles to go on the country road; in the winter it would have been dark before they got home. I'm sure my father had good reasons for not being there, but I'm sorry, Jack.

Our parents went to a lot of trouble so we could learn Japanese. Since others considered us Japanese and not so much American, they felt we

DOI: 10.5876/9781607322542:c04

should know the language. So Nihongo Gakko was a common experience for many Nisei. This doesn't mean we all became proficient; quite the contrary. Japanese is a difficult language that requires a lot more concentration and dedication than we brought to it. For most of us, Nihongo Gakko was how we spent our Saturdays or time after school; we did our required lessons, but it was a less pressurized respite from our regular school. Even our lunches were different. On Saturdays my mother would pack my lunch of *onigiri* (rice ball) or *makizushi* (sushi roll) or leftover *okazu* (cooked meat and vegetables) and other Japanese dishes I wouldn't dare take to the American school. Those lunches made Saturday school special.

We used to line up outside, standing at arm's length according to grade and height, and a monitor would command us to attention: "*kiotsuke*!" We would bow to the Sensei, who usually had a few words of greeting, after which the monitor would yell "*Susume*" (forward), and we would march inside in a fairly orderly fashion.

Since it was a one-room school, Sensei was in charge of many grades; while he attended to one grade, the rest of us were expected to study independently. This allowed for considerable levity in the classroom, and I remember Sensei constantly warning us to be quiet.

I think I had a kind of affinity for the language. I remember when I was about four, even before I could read, I would look at the Japanese section of the *Nichi Bei* newspaper and pick out all the characters with a roof over them and imagine them to be houses somehow connected with people; this actually wasn't too far-fetched.

Depending on the situation, I can say I'm halfway fluent; for a Nisei, I think I do pretty well. But after Nihongo Gakko, evening class during high school, advanced class in camp, and a BA in Oriental languages from UCLA, I should do better. What happened is that I would forget the characters and have to relearn them. After many repetitions of this process, some of the characters stuck with me, but I am far from literate. As for speaking the language, I wish I could speak like a native. It's such a pleasure to hear Japanese or any language spoken well. I'd like to live in Japan for a while, preferably in rural Japan where I would hear nothing but Japanese and be forced to speak it constantly. But this is only a dream I have.

Nihongo Gakko was where I picked up the acting bug. Every year there would be a Shugyoshiki, a promotional exercise, in which we demonstrated our progress in the use of the language. This would be in the form of stories, songs, and dances, providing parents with an evening of entertainment. One year Sensei, who was apparently a frustrated writer, wrote a hilarious comedy skit for our class, and the audience roared at everything I said and did on the stage. With that heady sensation and people telling me how good I was, I began to think I had a talent for acting—I've been acting off and on ever since. So my first acting experience was at Nihongo Gakko.

I wonder how much Nihongo Gakko helped in our communication with our parents. Most of us could communicate with them on a very basic level—what we learned as children before we began to speak English. Actually, we were needed in their interchange with hakujin. From the time I was eight or nine, I remember, I was the family's chief interpreter. Most Issei could carry on a simple conversation about the weather or health or crops with a hakujin; there would be much laughter to cover blind spots and for goodwill, and it helped that the hakujin spoke in a deliberate pidgin English. But whenever there was a problem (it was usually the hakujin who posed the problem) or a need for some negotiation, there would be a hurried call for me.

So there I would be, a kid of eight or so, standing between agitated or anxious adults—one a hakujin, always large and intimidating, and my father or mother or both, who didn't quite trust me though they were entirely dependent on me. It was a thankless job, especially when there was tension; then the anger and frustration seemed to come at me from both sides. As a bridge, I was also helping the hakujin, though I was never aware of that at the time. I was only aware of the difference, how big he was, how hairy, how loud and forceful.

By the time I was ten, I was also writing business letters for my father, putting down in English what he dictated in Japanese. I would like to see those letters now, though I don't recall that we had any problems with them except once a few years later when I was around fourteen. My father, for some reason he never made clear to me, had me mail back a postcard advertising a refrigerator showcase. Why he was interested in such a thing was a puzzle to me. It was still the Depression, and he was barely making ends meet in the store. I guess he was dreaming; we were expecting something in the mail with pictures of showcases when one day a dapper-looking hakujin breezed into the store.

"How are you, Mr. Kashiwagi?" he asked, shaking Father's hand. He wanted to know if he had pronounced the name correctly. I translated and Father nodded.

"Good, good, Mr. Kashiwagi," he said. Then he asked about our family, calling me "a fine young man," which almost won me over, I must admit. After extolling the family, he turned his attention to the store. "Fine store you have here," he said. The store wasn't exactly "fine." With limited funds, Father had furnished it with homemade fixtures.

"I'm glad you're buying a showcase from us; it's just the thing that would be perfect right here," he said, locating it where the counter was.

I translated this and Father said, "*Nani?*" (What?)

"I've got just the right showcase to put there," he said, rummaging in his briefcase for some brochures.

"*Matta, matta*" (wait, please), we said.

"Yes?"

"We're sorry, but we are not interested in buying a showcase."

Ignoring our comment, he continued, "I'll arrange it so you'll have a beautiful new refrigerator showcase right here within a week. What do you say?"

"Sorry, no."

"What's the matter? Are you worried about the payment? Well, don't worry, pay what you can now and the rest you can pay later."

"No, sorry."

"What d'ya mean 'no, sorry'?" he said loudly, suddenly changing his tone. He was no longer the friendly hakujin I thought he was. "You said you wanted to buy a showcase."

"We never said that."

"I don't understand this at all. You said you wanted to buy a showcase; that's why I came all the way out here from San Francisco."

"No, no."

"What d'ya mean 'no, no'? You are obligated to buy, you know."

I tried to translate this, but it was difficult; I was afraid Father might explode. Sure enough, before I could finish . . .

"*Deteike!*" (get out) he roared, pointing to the door. I didn't have to translate this; the hakujin left hurriedly, barely remembering to take his briefcase. But his parting shot was, "I'll be back." I worried about that, though Father said it was only a threat; I didn't want to go through another experience like it.

But what was worse was when Father called me an "*Ikujinashi*" (coward) and added "*nanimo yaku ni tatan*" (good for nothing). I was devastated; I thought I had done the best I could. I didn't realize he was still angry at the hakujin or maybe at himself for having started it all in the first place.

Perhaps this is why I've always felt my Japanese should be better.

Bento

The first bento I can remember is the one I used to take to kindergarten. My parents knew how I hated going to kindergarten, so they bribed me with a special "obento." There was a meat sandwich, usually ham; some kind of fruit; and a piece of cake or candy. The only thing is, I didn't get to eat much of it. Other kids got to it first; they were like animals. We were all Nisei; the only non-Nisei was the teacher. Everyone spoke English except me. So kindergarten was no picnic for me.

This reminds me of the bento Mama used to make for the community picnic, sponsored by the Japanese Association of Loomis. Several families would gather together on a canvas spread in the shade of an oak tree and share the bento each had brought. I remember Mama's fried chicken—small pieces of boned chicken dipped in batter and cooked in oil, the same oil in which she had cooked the *age* (fried bean cake). Very greasy by today's standards, but how good it was cold with onigiri (rice balls). I've learned recently that this was chicken *karaage*.

Once my father drank too much at the picnic and made a fool of himself, or so he thought. Although he was a proper man, he was popular

DOI: 10.5876/9781607322542.c05

with the women. As a fish peddler, they looked for him every week. Actually, I never realized that my parents were attractive until years later, when I was told by people who remembered them. Anyway, on that day Father went around carrying somebody else's child on his back and singing loudly, which was unheard of for him. Later, when he was teased unmercifully by his women customers, he vowed never to drink again, and he never did.

In high school, I stopped bringing bento and instead brought lunch, sandwiches and things, in a paper bag. In those days our lunches were not refrigerated, so I would carry this bag around for half a day until lunchtime. When I started getting hives, I decided it was the mayonnaise in the sandwiches, and I stopped taking lunch and ate in the school cafeteria. I don't know how I managed that because money was quite scarce, but I must have convinced my parents by showing them the large, angry welts all over my body.

One of the pleasures of traveling in Japan is eating bento on the train. On the bullet train from Osaka to Hiroshima, I had hot bento. By pulling a string attached to the box, I set off a steaming device, and in a matter of minutes I had hot lunch on the train. Luckily, I was able to read the instructions in Japanese.

Going to Wakayama on another trip, this time on the JR (Japan Railway), I bought a box of anago fish bento, a regional specialty. How wonderful that was—having Kishu (Wakayama) bento while listening to Kishu dialect on the train was like visiting with my parents again.

The bento for our San Francisco Buddhist temple fundraiser features chicken teriyaki, *barazushi*, and other good foods. Since I have helped with the teriyaki preparation, I know how labor-intensive it is. First, the quartered chicken is de-fatted and scrupulously cleaned, then washed carefully and dried, then salted lightly, dipped in egg, floured, and cooked in oil. Then it's brushed with a special sauce (the recipe is a secret), sprinkled with sesame seeds, baked in the oven for fifteen minutes, and cooled. That's our special chicken teriyaki bento, a San Francisco treat.

So I'm a pushover for bento—anywhere, any kind, anytime.

(Note: A version of this piece was originally written for the San Francisco Buddhist church bulletin as an ad for its chicken bento sale.)

Three Spanish Girls

When I was almost eight we moved to town—my parents had taken over the fish market/grocery store. One good thing about the move was that I didn't have to ride the bus to school and risk missing it going home, as I had once and the school principal had to drive me home. My parents didn't know what to make of that, but that's another story. This one is about walking to school, which took only ten minutes even with my tiny strides. I could also go home for lunch. So there was no more lunch pail to carry around and worry over. I must say I enjoyed walking to and from school until . . .

The three Spanish girls arrived on the scene.

They were big girls, many grades ahead of me. The three were always together. They would come to the store to buy candy, spending the few pennies they had. Many of the candies were a penny each, but the girls were fixed on the potato chips, which came in a small wax paper bag for a nickel. The three of them together were able to manage that. But the much larger bag they coveted cost a quarter, beyond their means. The bags of potato chips were hooked on a display rack.

Since our living quarters were in the back of the building, the store was often left unattended. Father installed a bell on the screen door that would alert us when someone came, and if I happened to be

DOI: 10.5876/9781607322542.c06

home I would call out "*Okyaku-san*" (customer) and Mother would drop whatever she was doing in the kitchen and hurry out to the front. One day, the Spanish girls somehow managed to silence the bell and entered stealthily. But when I heard a loud rustling noise, I called out "Mama" and Mother rushed out and caught one of the girls red-handed, holding the large bag of potato chips. The girls managed to escape; in their hurry and confusion, they left the bag of chips.

The next day, when I was walking back to school after lunch, I saw the three girls coming toward me. When they were near me, they bonded together and formed a wall, blocking my way, making me feel trapped like a small animal. I tried to get through, but I was blocked while the girls hooted and hollered in delight. Soon I began to cry; only after a while did they let me through.

They terrorized me in this way for almost a month, and I dreaded walking back to school after lunch. I tried to change the time of my walk by rushing or delaying my lunch, but the girls always seemed to know when I was coming. They would be there as though they had been waiting for me. To be fair, the girls never touched me, just frightened me half to death. I didn't tell anyone—not my parents or my teacher—what was happening. I suffered the terror alone.

Two of the girls were quite alike; I think they were sisters, maybe twins. The other girl was taller and more dominant. They were precocious girls, quite buxom and sexy. This, of course, was a later observation; at the time I just noticed that they had bright red lips and dark, flashing eyes and were always very loud, chattering in Spanish or what I guessed was Spanish.

Though the experience happened many years ago, when I was eight or so, the memory has remained with me through the years. I think it had a long-term effect on me; it certainly inhibited my development as a normal male. I did not feel comfortable with the opposite sex for many years; it wasn't until my late twenties that I slowly and tentatively began to relate to them.

Iros las tres españolas! Be gone, three Spanish girls!

Dominguez

From time to time, I find myself thinking about Dominguez Mendoza, wondering if he is still alive. I owe him a treat, a milkshake. It sounds silly, but it happened when I was fourteen.

At first, I couldn't tell Dominguez or anybody else from the twenty or more Filipino men out at the ranch. They all seemed alike to me—the same dark faces, the bandana neckerchiefs, the light, quick feet, and the Tagalog speech. Maybe we Japanese all seemed alike to them. I don't know.

Anyway, I kept away from them as much as I could, even though we were doing the same job, picking Santa Rosa plums. We even drank water from the same canteen, though none of the men drank half as much as I did.

I guess I was afraid of them. I had heard stories, and believed them, about how handy they were with knives and how they thought nothing of sticking one in a man's heart. Also, it did not sound too chummy, the way they talked back and forth—any minute I expected them to start slinging daggers or one of those trick knives people said they carried. Nothing like that ever happened, but I was always looking for it. I admit I was a little prejudiced in that respect, at least when I was fourteen.

DOI: 10.5876/9781607322542:c07

43

I suppose I learned much of that from my father. He always said, "You can't trust those Filipinos," and I believed him, for he had his troubles with them. He liked to have their trade selling them groceries, but the real challenge was getting paid. They practically bought out the store—a crate of this and that, vegetables, piles of canned goods, and pounds of fish. Everything was on credit, and about five of the men—leaders, I supposed, or men who could write—signed their names to the bill. Beautiful handwriting and names like music—Richard Bello, Carlos Esteban, Dominguez Mendoza; but darned if Father could remember them for a minute.

One summer the men forgot to pay. Father chased them all the way to Sacramento, but they got away easily, scattering to pool halls, hotels, bars, and other places. He lost nearly sixty dollars, which was quite a sum for a small store in those days. He got wise to them by asking their boss to give him early notice of payday so he could be around for his share. I guess he didn't have much trouble after that; I no longer saw him suddenly chasing off to Sacramento.

I didn't start to change my views until I got to know Dominguez. I was fourteen, and I could pick plums. I had picked them since I was ten years old. Every new season I had to learn all over again, but after a couple of days I could size the plums at a glance. I could tell which were packed five by fives, four by fives, and four by fours. I knew the colors, too. I knew what was half-color, quarter-color, straw-color, and green-color. I could also handle the eight-foot ladder better than anyone else. It was heavy but I didn't move it around much—just poked it in between the branches four or five places, and I had circled the tree and was moving on to the next.

"Always stay one tree ahead of the others," Father would say. He was interested in my work; he didn't want me fired. I did what he told me, even stayed two trees ahead sometimes, working hard whether the foreman was out of sight or standing right below me. When he was watching me, I probably worked even harder. The thought never occurred to me to relax once in a while, let the breeze cool off the sweat, or to take it easy climbing up the ladder instead of bounding up. I didn't smoke then, so I didn't waste any time rolling one either.

I had been working for about a week when one day Dominguez walked up alongside me on the way back to the fields.

"It is hot for you?" Dominguez asked.

"Sure is," I said. It was hell going back to work after lunch, the sun burning hot close above my head. I thought about being at home, sitting in the shade, nibbling on a piece of ice, and doing nothing. Five more hours seemed like a long time.

"Five hours to eternity," Dominguez said. I looked at him, thinking what a strange thing to say. His face was pockmarked. Many of the men were scary, with most of them in their twenties and thirties, but at that moment this guy was terrifying—there were pockmarks under his eyes, on his flat nose, all over his face. Then I noticed he was grinning and I forgot about the marks.

"What do you mean?" I asked.

He looked me in the eyes. "You are young. Half of the time you do not know what is what." Then he added wistfully, "You are very lucky."

I didn't know what he meant, and I kept thinking about it. I didn't exactly resent his comment, but I didn't like it either. I suppose I didn't know what was what. Dominguez smiled and shrugged.

He talked to me a lot for the rest of the day, but I didn't say much at first, being shy and afraid it would interfere with my work. Dominguez, in contrast, seemed intent on not letting work get in the way of a good conversation.

"*Trabajo con las manos.* I work with my hands," he said, surprising me with Spanish.

DOMINGUEZ

45

"You speak Spanish?" I asked, curious because I had had some Spanish in high school.

"Sure," he said. He told me he had gone to Spanish mission school and that he had to learn everything all over again in English when the Americans came.

It was itchy and hot, and every time I looked at Dominguez I wanted to scratch myself. It was the heavy sweatshirt he wore, the kind I didn't even wear in winter. Finally, I became too curious and asked how he could wear a sweatshirt in the heat.

"This," he said pulling on it, "is the best. Is hot inside and when the wind comes is cool. That," he said, pointing at my glaring white T-shirt, "is too hot." Then, still standing in the shade, he said, looking up at me on the ladder: "Take it easy, boy. You have a long time to live. We all get paid the same. How much you getting anyway?" he asked, kidding me.

"Thirty cents an hour," I said. I was told not to tell anyone, but by now I was telling Dominguez almost anything. I knew the men were getting thirty-five cents an hour.

"Thirty cents? That is not right."

I got laid off before the pear season started, and I was happy. I didn't care for money. If I had a quarter on Sunday, I had a good time; I might go to Roseville to see a movie or go to a local baseball game, which didn't cost anything. Father didn't like it when I told him I was let go. He asked me why, and I couldn't tell him. I knew I hadn't done anything wrong. I had worked hard, but he wasn't convinced until the boss told him he had to cut his crew and didn't want to fire any of the Filipinos for fear the whole gang might leave. He also told him that he hated to let me go because I was a good worker, which satisfied Father.

I didn't get to loaf for long. When it came to finding work for me, Father was a hustler. He took all the money I earned, too, and used it to appease his creditors. He was always worrying about his creditors, cursing them, and I guess I helped him out a little, though he never told me so.

Two days later I was working on a big pear ranch.

Fruit season was finally over, and I was enjoying the end of my summer vacation, when I was sure Father couldn't find work for me, even if he begged the farmers. Only then could I really take it easy.

The only problem was, school was starting in a week. All summer long I had wanted school to start, and now I hated the thought of it.

One day I spotted Dominguez across the street near Stevens Drug Store and waved to him, calling out his name. He motioned me to come over, and I ran across the street. We shook hands and talked like old friends. He had on a chalk-striped green suit, which I thought was classy, though maybe a bit loud for a man his age.

"Say, I promised you a treat on that real hot day, remember?" he said.

"Yeah," I said, all smiles.

"Where can we get a milkshake?"

"Over here at Stevens Drug Store," I said eagerly. It was the only place that had a soda fountain.

"Suppose Stevens is all right?" Dominguez asked.

"Sure, he's all right. Come on." I led him into the store.

Two women looked at us curiously, but I didn't care. I knew they came to the drugstore every day in a different dress for their newspapers or sedatives or whatever. I used to watch the goings-on at Stevens Drug Store from my parents' store across the street. I often wondered if that was all they had to do, drive to town once a day.

We got up on the stools and waited to be served. Mr. Stevens seemed busy chatting with the ladies while we waited. It wasn't that Mr. Stevens didn't know me; sometimes I delivered packages for him, and he gave me a choice of a dime or a soda. (Naturally, I took the soda.) Finally, the women left, and Mr. Stevens came to wait on us. He glanced at me and then at Dominguez, where his eyes rested for a moment and then shifted back to me.

"A strawberry shake," I ordered, and the druggist lifted the heavy lid of the ice cream compartment and started digging.

"What're you going to have?" I asked Dominguez, and he shrugged his shoulders. I watched Mr. Stevens pour milk in the can and wanted to tell him to take it easy with the milk—I liked my milkshakes rich and thick.

"Please give me a strawberry milkshake," Dominguez said in his precise English.

The druggist was hooking the can on the shaking machine, and his back was turned. "We don't serve any liquor here." It wasn't too clear, but that's what I thought he said. Talking to himself, I supposed. Then he turned around and, looking straight at Dominguez, he repeated, the words popping out of the corner of his mouth: "We don't serve any liquor here." At the time, I didn't know what he meant; I looked to Dominguez.

Dominguez didn't look back at me. He just handed me a half-dollar; his palm was sticky. I watched him go outside and his green suit seemed somehow faded, the coat drooping loosely over his round shoulders.

Mr. Stevens poured my order in a glass. I still didn't understand what had happened. It wasn't until later that I realized what Mr. Stevens was saying. I should have asked the druggist why he didn't serve my friend. I should have made him admit his prejudice, at least make him squirm a little. I should have walked out with Dominguez and never come back. I should have known better. But like a dumb kid, I paid and just drank the milkshake quietly.

I didn't mess with straws; I took it straight from the glass as I had seen others do. And I choked. I guess I tried to drink it too fast. The milkshake wasn't as good as I had expected anyway.

When I got my change and went outside, Dominguez was sitting on a bench, looking at a newspaper. I could tell he wasn't reading because he didn't have his glasses on.

"Thanks a lot, Dominguez," I said, trying to give him the change. He shook his head and lifted his face toward me. He did that a lot when he talked, and I knew what he meant. "Gee, thanks," I said pocketing the coins.

"How was the milkshake?"

"It was swell," I lied, "but what happened?"

Dominguez didn't look sore, just kind of sad. He was quiet for a moment, then he said, "You mean in there?" indicating with his head. "Oh, I didn't feel like drinking a milkshake."

"But," I started to say, and he interrupted me. "You know, boy, sometimes it is easier for me to get a glass of beer in a saloon."

"I don't know what you mean."

Dominguez winked at me. "You are young. Half of the time you do not know what is what." Then he added sadly, "You are lucky."

I wanted to ask him a few more questions, but the Greyhound bus came and Dominguez picked up his suitcase and boarded the bus without saying anything to me. "So long, Dominguez," I called, waving when I saw him by the window. He grinned. Funny, but I no longer noticed the pockmarks on his face, just his sad grin. The bus roared away. I never saw Dominguez after that.

It's been many years now. I didn't understand what Dominguez was trying to tell me until later in my life. Too bad I couldn't return Dominguez's treat. He's probably gone by now, sweet old guy. Meeting Dominguez, I learned that Filipinos are nothing like the monsters people told stories about. I also learned that there are people out there like Mr. Stevens—too many, in fact.

I haven't been back to Stevens Drug Store in a long time. I wonder if they still don't sell liquor there.

I Will Go and Return

"I will go and return . . . *itte kaerimasu*," the little boy said, repeating the Japanese expression he had learned a few days before. Even now, I can't forget how he seemed to know that the expression is followed by some movement away, for after each time he said it he would wheel his tricycle around and drive off—to school, to work, to town, or wherever else his imagination might take him. Soon he will be saying it every morning as he goes off to school, and it will become a part of his growing up. But, like me, he will not realize the true meaning of the expression until later in life.

I used to be like this boy. I must have said it thousands of times, never with much thought, until one time when I was seventeen years old: itte kaerimasu. "I will go and return." And I don't think I really said it again after that.

I remember how on that day my father sat smoking and brooding in his rocking chair. He had been to town that morning and was unusually quiet after his return. Their store had been closed for a few years, and Dad and Mom had been moving around, staying with friends,

DOI: 10.5876/9781607322542.c08

sharecropping an occasional harvest. I was home from Los Angeles, where I spent my last year of high school.

He coughed sometimes as he rocked; Mother looked up from her mending when he did. Finally he spoke: "I met a man in town who was recruiting men for the grape harvest. I told him I would go if I could." He stopped to cough, then added above a hoarse whisper, "I'd kill myself if I went."

Suddenly, I was afraid. I wanted to leave the room, but before I could do anything Father asked, "You will go to the harvest?" His voice was deep, gentle, yet firm.

"No, Papa, no!" I wanted to cry out. I was eager to continue my education; going to the harvest would mean I couldn't go to college. It was true that I had no special ambition at the time, but while I was at school I could forget about working the hot summer days in the orchard, the meager rations on the table, and the shanty-like house we lived in. I was a lot like the other students in that respect. I didn't answer Father's question. Father, too, was silent.

I gazed out the window and saw the high pile of horse manure, and I thought of the animal in the barn. Beyond the dung, in the distance, the plum trees looked light and carefree, their branches again springing upward toward the sky. Those were the trees, I thought, that promised so much in the spring, that demanded so much work from us in the summer, that brought only disappointment in the fall. I wanted to run out to the orchard and shake down the leaves and pull up the trees one by one.

Then I remembered the boss who owned the trees; in fact, who owned everything—the orchard, the house, the barn, the horse. But father liked working for the boss, who every once in a while rewarded him with a cigar. I think it was because of their mutual regard for work that the two men got along so well—the boss who didn't work and Father who did the work, who practically lived for it.

He began to cough again, and I noticed that Mother not only stopped mending but stopped breathing as well. Father wasn't old in terms of years, but by the kind and amount of work he had done he was very old. He was also sick with TB.

"Papa, I will go to the harvest," I said.

"Good," he nodded, and we looked at each other. Although his arms did not reach out for me or mine to him, at that moment we were closer to each other than we had ever been. Not only was I the son, but I was the father, too. He began to tell me things about himself; I would recall them later in my life, grow to associate them not only with my father but with myself as well.

He had promised his father that he would not return to Japan until he was rich and successful, but that had not been important to his father. "Just take care of yourself," his father had said to Father, who wasn't even twenty at the time.

Over the years, he was a railroad hand, migrant laborer, truck farmer, fisherman, restaurant owner, grocer, and tenant farmer. At twenty-nine he married, sending for Mother from Japan, and in five years he was the father of three children.

He coughed again, and his expression changed. "It hurts me to see you go," he said. "I worked hard hoping you children could go to school and at least get a good start in life. Now you have to go work in fields like I did. It is like turning the calendar back thirty years."

"I don't mind going," I said.

"That's good. Maybe in two or three years things will change and you'll be able to continue school."

We began to pack. I spread out a sheet of canvas on the floor, and on it I piled a quilt and some blankets. Then Mother brought an armload of work clothes from the family dresser, and I arranged them neatly so I could roll them into a bundle.

"Here, let me do it," Father said, taking the rope from me. "There's a way to do this, and I ought to know. Nothing is more revealing of a man's character than the look of his bundle. Usually, a man with a sloppy roll is a lazy, loud-talking man, the first to be fired," he said, tying the bundle neatly and expertly.

Then Father brought out his suitcase. It was old and battered; the stiff brown leather was scarred and scratched. "When I bought this in Japan I said to myself, 'As soon as I get to America I'll toss it back in the ocean.' I never dreamed that one day my own son would be taking the same suitcase. Well, it's getting old, but it'll do, it'll have to do." I didn't like to hear him talk like that, and I was glad when he gruffly ordered me to hurry and finish packing.

The man who told Father about the job was coming for me in the afternoon, so after lunch I put the blanket roll and the suitcase out on the porch. Father took out his wallet and slipped me a five-dollar bill.

"Here, take this," he said. Mother, who happened to be watching, asked, "Why, Papa?"

"Don't worry, Mama. It's all right."

"You spend it wisely." Mother turned to me, knowing it was useless talking to Father.

"Sure, Mama," I said.

"Don't keep bad company, and don't go into town all the time," she warned.

"Oh, Mama, leave him alone. He'll take care of himself. He's going to do a man's work, and a man's got to have some fun. You spend it any way you like," he said to me, but I knew it was more in jest toward Mother. "Yes, Papa, you should know. You were such a fool before I came," she said. I was enjoying the fuss they were making over me.

Soon, a shiny new car drove up to the house. The stranger, dressed in a white shirt, neatly pressed pants, and a Panama hat, helped me load the things in the trunk compartment. Then, bowing to my parents, I said, "I will go and return." Itte kaerimasu.

Father grunted, smiling a little, and Mother told me to take care and to write. I got in the car and turned around as we drove away. Through the rear window I saw the figures of my parents standing in front of the porch, before the rose trellis that shaded the dingy rooms inside. As we left, I had a feeling that I was seeing them for the last time.

Soon, we were on the highway. "How do you feel, young man? You're leaving home for the harvest for the first time, aren't you?" the stranger beside me asked. I didn't say anything, and the man laughed to fill the silence. I rolled down the window and let the wind hit my face. The walnut trees along the highway raced by as the car gained speed. The trees seemed like man and woman, man and woman, and I said to myself, "I will go and return. I will go and return . . ."

When the harvest was over I went back, and I left home for work many times after that. Yet, thinking back now, it seems as though I have never been back, that from that day of my seventeenth year I have been leaving and leaving . . .

Itte kaerimasu. "I will go and return, Daddy," the boy was saying again, and I nodded and followed him out of the room. I heard him repeat the expression, and I was again the seventeen-year-old boy whispering into the wind, "I will go and return." But after a moment, I found myself calling out "Be careful, son," as the boy drove his tricycle down the dimly lit hallway.

After Supper

It was after supper. A few men had filed out of the kitchen door, wiping the sweat off their hot faces with a red or blue bandana. Some had finished supper and were sitting in the shade on a stray cot or empty lug boxes.

"It sure is hot," one man said.

"Eating in that hot room is like working in the field," another man said.

"It's the August heat, same every year," a solemn-faced man said.

After a loud and long conversation with the female cook, the last man stumbled out of the kitchen. He was a small man. His round face was red.

"It's damn hot!" he shouted as he ambled over to the group and slumped on a lug box.

"Your heat is from the wine," someone said.

"That's right," the little man agreed instantly. "I took a long snort after work and two more coffee cups during supper," he said and snickered as though he had committed some devilish act.

"There's a good crop of Tokays this year, but it's still a little early," the solemn-faced man said.

"Yeah, it's still too early," the little man said, as though it was his cue. He struck a match and without lighting the cigarette he continued,

DOI: 10.5876/9781607322542:c09

"There's no color on the grapes." The force of his hot breath snuffed out the flickering light. He fumbled in his pocket for another match and went on, "The boss wants us to pick a lot, so I go and pick the green, sour grapes and stick 'em in the bottom. And what happens? The inspector comes out to the field and turns over four of my boxes. 'No. 9 is too green. Who's No. 9?' he shouts so everyone could hear. I'm hiding in the vine acting like I'm working, but he comes and points at me and says, 'You, No. 9, be more careful.' 'No can help,' I tell him."

He struck another match, and just as he was about to light up again, he stopped. What he had to say seemed more urgent, and he took the cigarette out of his mouth.

"Now he's got his eye on my number. He'll kick about No. 9 all the time." Momentarily, he was silent. Then he said again, "I'll change my number. Sure, that's what I'll do. I'll change my number. That'll fool him," he said, laughing, but he alone laughed. He noticed the silence for the first time.

"Why so quiet? Where's the life? Let's have a game of poker," he suggested. There was no answer.

"You men are dead," the little man sneered. He got up and staggered away, shouting, "Poker! Poker!" Such a call on Saturday nights was like a mating call. It brought eager men hurrying to the gaming table. But it wasn't Saturday, and no one moved. No one seemed interested.

A slight breeze caused a faint rustling of the poplar leaves. "It's getting cooler," one man said, and the others agreed. Each man smoked his pipe, cigarette, or Bull Durham. Smoking was a thing of habit, but it had its purposes. They called it "one smoke." In the field "one smoke" meant a pause, a brief respite from the labor. The field boss did not object, or at least he didn't say anything because "one smoke" was accepted in all the labor camps. But there was no pleasure like the pleasure of "one smoke" after supper. The tobacco had a special taste unknown to many other smokers. It was one of their few pleasures but a priceless one.

The men sat back. They seemed occupied with their thoughts. No one spoke. None dared to voice his thoughts. It was sentimental stuff, something they would laugh at. It was personal and private. But the thoughts were identical in every mind:

"I was tired and hungry in the field today. My legs were heavy, and my back ached. I said 'To hell with grape picking, to hell with work.' The hours were long and the sun was hot . . . now the day is over. I'm home. I took a bath and had a good supper. I made eight dollars today. I'm sitting and smoking.

"This feeling I have now is hard to describe in words. Men who do a hard day's work know what it's like. The rich and idle can never know. This joy is like a song. It is a song, my song. And no one can take it away, not even the Chinese gambling house. I hear this song at the end of each working day. It is not a part of day or night, there is no overlapping; it is a short, separate period removed from time when I hear it.

"The moment of song is brief. It cannot be long, just tonight when I'm alone—alone in bed, without a woman, without a wife, without children, just myself in the darkness of the bunkhouse that is my home, where the song will soon fade. If it is long, I think of the years ahead when I'm old and sick and can no longer work. I think of myself unwanted, alone, waiting for the day to die, glad to die, when the song will finally be gone. This period must be brief for the joy to ring, just a fleeting moment . . . I hear it now. It is a good song, my song, the song of my life, one I made in the field today."

It got fairly dark, and the mosquitoes began to buzz around. One by one the men got up and, without a word, turned into the bunkhouse, myself among them.

New Year's Eve, 1940

That night, my brother sat at the table listening to the radio the boss had given us for Christmas. Since we were on the West Coast, he had already listened to programs on the year's major news events and heard the crowds in New York and Chicago welcome in the New Year. Now the radio was tuned to a program coming directly from a party in some fancy hotel in San Francisco. I don't think he liked this for he kept switching stations; but everywhere people were doing the same thing—drinking, dancing, making a lot of noise—and it was hard to say which was more sentimental, the music or the announcer's comments. This wasn't part of our year-end tradition, yet my brother kept the radio on, though very faintly so we were hardly aware of it. I think it was his way of expressing his discomfort regarding the uneasy silence in the room.

Having bathed already, we were in pajamas, robes, and slippers. Now our mother and sister were taking their traditional year-end baths, washing away the old year's dirt and grime. The house, too, was clean—the ceiling swept of cobwebs, the floors scrubbed, and the windows washed. Even the woodstove looked new, with a coat of black polish. The wood box was filled, and more chopped wood was piled neatly on the front porch. My brother and I had spent a good part of the morn-

DOI: 10.5876/9781607322542:c10

ing sawing and chopping the deadwood from the fruit trees we had hauled in from the orchard.

The beds were made up with clean linens, and our mother and sister had everything prepared for the traditional New Year's Day meal. They had finished rather early, since no guests were expected and the celebration would be very quiet. But at midnight we would have the soba (buckwheat) noodles, which symbolized long life, and in the morning there would be the ceremonial breakfast of rice cake soup (*ozoni*), herring roe, seaweed, and soybeans. A big bottle of sake (rice wine) was on the back porch just in case somebody should drop by.

How different it was from a few years ago, when Father would be out all day making his rounds and Mother would be kept busy entertaining the callers who came one after another. The bottle of sake would be constantly warming in the pot, and Mother would have to replenish the tray of artfully arranged food many times during the day.

Then people stopped making New Year calls; instead, a party was arranged at the community hall where everyone could meet at once. The parties were not scheduled on the first day of the year, as it was customary for the women to stay inside on New Year's Day, when they were needed to serve the men. So the parties were usually held a week or so later, on a Sunday.

By then, Father, though still retaining membership in the community groups, rarely attended the meetings and didn't go to the parties. He had been well liked and respected and had many friends, but now he stayed at home, rarely going to town. Mother, Brother, and I did the shopping and tended to the necessary business. We had few visitors, and I think Father, who was fond of people, missed them. But the most painful part was that this isolation was forced upon him by his illness. He spent much of his time reading the newspaper and old magazines.

On this night, he sat on a stool by the side of the stove that stood in the corner of the room. The red glow on his cheeks was from the heat, but the color in his face was always there, a sign of his illness. He coughed now and then, mostly in his throat, but at night we heard him coughing a lot in his room. He sat quietly, almost morosely, his mind far away.

I wished he would talk; then we would gather around him and listen. I remembered nothing better than sitting around the stove and listening to Father, not saying much ourselves, only something now and then to show our interest.

"Papa, Papa." I wanted to reach out to him but checked the impulse. The distance between us was becoming something more than physical; I was rapidly losing sight of Father, what he really meant to us.

My sister was the only one who could talk naturally with him. Sometimes she got very close to him, touching him, even though Father always tried to keep a safe distance. I wondered if she knew that he had TB.

On the radio Guy Lombardo was playing some sickly music, and I wanted to tell my brother to turn it off, but the announcer in his cheerful voice said there were only twenty minutes left in the old year.

On New Year's Eves past, Father would give us his review of the year, beginning with something about the outside world—some national or international event that had impressed him. Then he would talk about our progress in school or recall something we did that in his words was a major achievement. He didn't dwell on our failures; failures are for adults, he would say, critically considering his own year and shaking his head when he had not measured up to his expectations. But always he was thankful for our health and the goodwill of our friends, and Mother would nod and say "Yes, Papa."

Mother and Sister came in laughing and chatting, their faces radiant and for a moment looking more like sisters. Mother bowed toward Father without speaking. She was always apologetic about bathing before he did; it was unheard of for a woman to bathe before a man did, and she could never get used to the idea of upstaging her husband.

NEW YEAR'S EVE, 1940

63

But Father insisted, and she obeyed. He was giving up so many privileges because of his illness that we were especially careful to follow his wishes when he voiced them, trying to preserve what authority he retained.

"We stirred up the fire so the bath should be nice and hot, Papa," my sister said brightly. Father grunted, got up, and went into his room; a draft of cold air rushed into the room before he could close the door behind him. Soon he came out in his robe; after making sure the door was closed, he went out to the bathhouse.

"Why must we go on like this?" I wanted to cry out, but when I looked at Mother she seemed to read my thoughts and her eyes said, "No, no." She turned away and left the room. It was always like that.

For a year now, no one had been permitted to go into Father's room. Mother didn't go in there, not even at night, for they had stopped living as man and wife long ago. At first we couldn't accept this, but gradually, we also became fearful of going into the room, thinking the air inside was terribly contaminated.

From bits of conversation I overheard, I knew that Mother had tried to get Father to go to the sanatorium, and he had refused. Mother did not tell us about this. Father had been to the doctor, yet nothing was said to us. The illness was kept a secret between them, and we didn't feel we should broach something so closely guarded.

Meanwhile, Mother kept Father's rice bowls, chopsticks, dishes, and cups separate and soaked them in boiling water after each use. She washed his clothes and bed linens separately. This is how we first guessed that Father was sick.

Mother also became careful that Father didn't strain himself at work, which meant we all had to work harder to make ends meet. As a sharecropper, Father was only responsible to see that the work was done on time, so he wasn't under any pressure to put in a full day's work if he wasn't feeling well. He could rest when he tired or take a nap in the afternoon. Mostly, he supervised the work and Mother did what she could, and my brother and I took care of the heavy work after school and on weekends. When there was a special job that took several days in a row, like spraying the pear trees, Father tried to plan it during a school holiday; if rain or engine trouble on the spray rig disrupted this schedule, then we stayed home from school to do the job. He seemed anxious to leave all his knowledge of farming to us, as if he knew he might not be around much longer.

When Father came back in, we all went into the kitchen, where Mother had readied the traditional New Year's Eve soba.

"The noodles smell good, Mama," Father said, a note of cheer in his voice. It was the first time he had spoken all evening, and our spirits lifted as we took up the chopsticks. Then the announcer on the radio said there were only five minutes left in the old year, except he said the bearded old man would be leaving forever in another five minutes. We heard the bell tolling in the distance, and we stopped eating and listened. I knew the bell was being struck by the people attending the service at the temple, each one taking turns until the bronze bell had been struck 108 times, as was the Buddhist custom.

"It's to drive away evil thoughts," my brother said.

"No, they represent human passions," my sister said.

"They represent the truths," I said. Mother, who was about to say something, raised her hand to her mouth. The ringing continued and Father said, "It's to remind us of all our weaknesses."

When we finished eating the noodles Father said, "That was very good, Mama," and Mother seemed pleased by the rare praise. The bell continued to toll; suddenly, there was an explosion from the radio and the announcer was shouting "Happy New Year!" A siren went off, someone fired a gun, and there was honking of horns.

"It's the New Year," Father said, making it official in our house. "There's something I want to say to you," he said before we could rise to greet him. "In a few days I'm going to arrange to go to the sanatorium. I think you can manage without me. Mama and the boys can take care of the ranch, and you'll help too, won't you?" he asked my sister. "Yes, of course, Papa," she said, answering first for the rest of us, even Mother, who seemed surprised by the announcement.

Then Father did something very unusual. He ordered Mother to get the ceremonial wine cup; Mother, without the slightest hesitation, bowed and fetched it from the cupboard. After washing it, she placed it next to the bottle of sake my sister had brought in from the front porch. The cup was quite large, almost the size of a rice bowl; its rather ornate design was crackled. Mother poured some sake and, holding the cup in both hands, raised it toward Father, who took it and drank. At a signal from Father, Mother poured more sake, then handed the cup to me. It was an ancient ritual that began with the samurai—by drinking out of the same cup, an unbreakable bond was established between the lord and his retainers. It had been all but forgotten in our family, and I wondered why Father was reviving it now. But there was no time for idle thoughts as the cup was extended. I took it in my hands and drank, then passed it to my brother, who also took a sip. When my mother and sister had drunk from the cup, all four of us, out of some strange force of tradition, bowed in unison toward Father. With our heads bowed, we received his New Year's greeting.

Then he said, "We have a fine family, Mama." Mother tried to smile bravely, and for a moment I thought she was going to hug us like the time, years ago, when she had embraced the three of us after our little sister had died of TB meningitis—but she didn't. We were not a physically demonstrative family. But somehow I knew we were together, bonded in a warm embrace, one that included my father.

NEW YEAR'S EVE, 1940

Papa's Hat

It's an ordinary felt hat, brown, and not stiff like cardboard that would crack with age. Though inexpensive, the felt must have been of good quality. There was enough suppleness that I could reshape it into a porkpie hat, as I did when I decided to start wearing it. I thought the high crown wasn't right for a young man, a college student, which I was at the time. So I decided to reshape it to suit myself.

Papa had bought the hat at the J. C. Penney store in Roseville, where we bought all our clothing when I was growing up. It was his dress-up hat, except that he didn't have many occasions to dress up. As it turned out, he wore it mainly to funerals. He never wore it for work. If he had, I'm sure his women customers would have been disappointed, even upset that he wasn't the affable fish peddler in his worn cap and striped overalls. So the hat remained in the closet, mostly unworn and quite new.

I know Papa hadn't taken it with him to the sanatorium, where he spent the war years as a tuberculosis patient. During the hectic days when we had to pack everything in a hurry, Mama must have thrown the hat into the trunk along with the family photographs, books in Japanese, her silk kimono, letters from relatives in Japan—things we couldn't take with us to camp. The trunk was stored in the Buddhist temple and was delivered to us later when we were in Tule Lake.

DOI: 10.5876/9781607322542:c11

The hat caught my eye as soon as I opened the trunk. I knew it was Papa's hat, but I wanted it for myself. I felt it belonged to me as the firstborn in the family, though Papa was still alive then.

But there is another reason I treasure the hat. I wore it when I was a student at UCLA in the early 1950s, despite the fact that no one on campus was wearing hats. At first, I wore my porkpie hat only when it rained, but as I became more comfortable with it, I started wearing it every day. I wasn't trying to make a fashion statement, though I noticed that more and more students were soon wearing some kind of headgear.

My purpose was to use the hat as a shield against other students. I didn't want anyone prying into my past. I took this aggressive, antisocial stance especially toward other Japanese American students. I thought, once they learned of my past, they would make me the object of scorn. Many in the community were making former Tule Lake people scapegoats, the "bad guys" or "disloyal Americans" or "troublemakers" who had been held in the notorious Tule Lake Segregation Center for defying the loyalty registration order.

Apparently my plan worked because no one came near me. It was as if I had a bad case of body odor. I rushed from class to class, took lunch by myself, and studied in a carrel in the library. But there was a downside to all this: I had no social life to speak of, which probably explains my late marriage.

At any rate, one white student in my advanced Japanese class, an oddity himself, kept eyeing me. One day he stopped me outside class.

"That's quite a hat you're wearing," he said. I noticed he was with a Japanese girl.

"You like it?"

"Yeah, it's okay."

"It belonged to my father. Of course, I changed the shape to suit myself," I said. This was more information than I had divulged to anyone. He and his girlfriend smiled. Then he said, "We've been wondering about you."

"So?"

"Why you're so different. Why you don't hang around with the others."

"Maybe I'm antisocial," I said, cutting off the conversation.

After that we talked occasionally, though we didn't become friends.

But more than anything, the hat represents to me who my father was. As a young man he had been an apprentice to his uncle, a Shingon priest in Wakayama. But one day he quit abruptly. He had been forced to marry against his will; after a few miserable days he left his bride, and the marriage was annulled. Soon after that he left for America. He wasn't quite twenty when he landed in Seattle.

His elder brother, who was already here, encouraged him to go to the Methodist church, where he could learn English from one of the Christian ladies. Father didn't like the idea of kneeling and praying, so what English he knew was learned outside of church and school.

He first worked as a section hand on the railroad. Because he was bigger than the others, he was made a foreman of the gang. He then worked on a hay ranch, baling hay. That was hard work, he always said. Then he worked his way down the state of California, picking fruit in the summer and pruning trees in the winter.

On a truck farm in Oxnard, he learned to drive a team of horses. That's when he developed a lifelong passion for horses, one I inherited. He became a fisherman, fishing for tuna out of Terminal Island. This was before radio and the aid of the US Coast Guard in an emergency, and he had many tales of harrowing experiences on the sea. In Los Angeles he ran a small café with a partner.

Around this time he sent for my mother, who came as a picture bride. They settled in Florin, near Sacramento, where they grew strawberries on a rented plot of land. I was born in Sacramento, delivered by a midwife. My two siblings came soon after.

Later, he was a sharecropper on a plum and peach ranch in Loomis. To get around, he bought a Model-T Ford. I remember riding in it to go to town, to visit friends, or to go as far as Sacramento, about thirty miles away.

His last enterprise was the fish market, which he bought in 1928. It was around this time that he purchased the hat. Was that a sign of prosperity? He also bought a new Model-A Ford panel built especially for his business of delivering fish and groceries. Then came the crash of 1929, and hard times followed. Only when he was hospitalized for pleurisy in 1933 did he give up the business. After recuperating for two years he resumed the business, but by then he had developed tuberculosis and his active life was over.

Papa's been gone for well over half a century. Only the hat remains. The hat is quite frail now; the band is frayed. But I like the soft feel of the felt, the sweat stains on the sweatband . . .

Kashiwagi, age one, with mother, Kofusa, 1923

Kashiwagi family, circa 1929. *Left to right*: Hiroshi, age seven, Fukumatsu, Kofusa, Eiko, and Ryo

(*Top row, fourth from the right*) Kashiwagi, age eight, with third-grade class, 1930

"Cap Boys of Loomis." Kashiwagi (*standing*), age nine, with Mikio Konda, Ryo Kashiwagi, and Fumio Kubo, 1931

Fukumatsu Kashiwagi, circa 1931, Loomis, California

Kashiwagi, age fifteen, at his family's store in Loomis with Fumio Kubo,
1937

Kashiwagi, age sixteen, with fellow honor roll students, circa 1938

Kashiwagi, age nineteen, in the fields with Hiroshi Hiura, 1941

Kashiwagi, age twenty-two, at Tule Lake, 1944

Kashiwagi, age twenty-three, as block manager at Tule Lake Segregation
Center, circa 1945

PART II

Little Theater in Camp

❧

I mentioned before that camp was exciting, at least at first. I was nineteen years old and eager for new adventures. There were all these new people of different and interesting backgrounds to meet. Strangely, camp gave me a chance to pursue what interested me the most: writing and acting, performing in front of people. I had taken a drama course at Dorsey High School during my year in Los Angeles and had acted in plays at the Japanese-language school. But nothing like the Little Theater at Tule Lake.

It was late summer 1942; we had only been in camp for about two months and already the camp newsletter, the *Tulean Dispatch*, was in operation. I noticed that announcements for recreational activities abounded. I guessed the administration was urging everyone to get involved in some activity to ward off boredom and depression among the inmates.

One of the announcements was an appeal for people interested in forming a theater, so I went to the first meeting and was surprised at the large turnout, about fifteen people. How exciting that was! Two persons assumed leadership roles: Perry Saito of the Recreation Department, who was the organizer, and Sada Murayama, a woman a bit older and more sophisticated than the rest of us, who seemed to

DOI: 10.5876/9781607322542.c12

have had some theater experience. She would direct the plays. Perry stated that the group was open to anyone interested in theater, experienced or not. The main purpose was to put on shows as diversions and entertainment for camp inmates. As for acting, we would learn together by actually being in plays and performing before an audience.

The recreation hall in Block 4 became our little theater. Thanks to the "behind-the-scenes people," we soon had a stage and a curtain at one end of the barrack and benches for the audience. Lights were made by using empty tin cans procured from the mess halls.

A program of three one-act plays was planned, and auditions for the parts were held. The first play bill included *Ile* by Eugene O'Neill, a comedy, and a fantasy. I was cast in the fantasy. The play featured Yukio Shimoda, who was primarily a dancer at the time and who would later become an actor on Broadway and in the movies. I played the *Maker of Dreams* (the title of the play) who was responsible for the romance between Yukio, as Pierrot, and a young lady, as Pierrette. It was definitely not a stellar role.

But my luck changed unexpectedly when one of the actors in the comedy decided to leave camp and I was chosen as an emergency replacement. So there I was with two parts, one of which I had to learn in a hurry as we were well into rehearsals. I had great fun playing a very proper clergyman in the comedy. It seemed the more serious I was with the character, the more laughs I got. Howard Imazeki, a journalist from San Francisco, praised my performance in his review for the *Tulean Dispatch*. This proved to be my first notice as an actor.

The most dramatic play was *Ile*, an early work by O'Neill. Perry Saito was the captain of the whaling ship. With murky lighting and the sound effects of a foghorn, a brooding sea atmosphere was created in which the bleak drama takes place.

After two years at sea, the crew of the icebound ship is ready to mutiny unless they head home, but the captain is determined to fill the ship with "Ile" (oil) first. The captain's wife, also homesick, pleads with him and finally convinces him to turn back. Just then a cry is heard that the ice has broken, and the captain, disobeying his promise to his wife, orders the ship forward. This is too much for the wife; her breakdown is enacted by the actress in her manic, disjointed playing of the organ. I have always wondered what happened to the woman who played the wife. She was electrifying.

The theater's capacity was around 150, and each performance was scheduled for a certain section (ward) of the camp. I believe we had seven or eight evening performances of each program.

The theater had its heyday during late 1942, and I was having a ball playing all kinds of interesting parts. Once I was cast as a convict on death row in the play *The Valiant*. It was definitely a major role—a man who goes to his death speaking lines from Shakespeare: "Cowards die many times before their deaths; the valiant never taste of death but once..."

One night I was told there were some people from Loomis in the audience, and I thought, wow, they're here to support me, a hometown kid. I'd better not screw up. Well, I heard later that they had come to check out how I was smoking onstage, whether I was faking it. Smoking was big in camp; everyone was starting the habit. I wasn't a smoker then when I was learning the part, but I was determined to look natural, as though I had been smoking for years. I think I rehearsed that more than anything else. Actually, smoking was crucial in the play—the convict's final cigarette before his execution. Unfortunately, goaded by other smokers, I did pick up the habit, which lasted for over twenty years.

In addition to directing the plays, Sada Murayama, an attractive matron, brought a touch of glamour before every performance when she stepped in front of the curtain—her eyes sparkling in the light— greeted the audience, and introduced the plays. Murayama, in fact, was the mother of the girl I would "save" from the American River after our release from camp.

Occasionally, when I wasn't onstage, I went out front to be part of the audience. When Sada Murayama concluded her introduction and the lights went down, I could sense the audience's anticipation. The moment before the curtains parted, before the lights came up—that magical moment was there in camp, too. Then the show began and no matter how crude the set, how untrained the performers, the audience was transported to another realm and a brief respite from reality. I was proud to be a part of that.

I don't recall the camaraderie within the group. I guess it was my nature. I've always been shy and introverted, quiet and observing, and rather awkward in social situations. It was the acting that concerned me, the chance to perform in front of people, to be the focus of their attention. That's when I was my true self before receding into my shell like a tortoise. What I *do* like is the give-and-take in acting; it's like a game without the rivalry. But there are rules, unwritten or otherwise: actors should give as well as take, have respect for each other, and NO UPSTAGING.

One day a man named Garrett Starmer appeared at our rehearsal. He was part of the Caucasian staff. He had appeared on Broadway and was soon giving the actors much-needed pointers on acting and suggesting changes in the direction of the plays. Then he volunteered to participate in one of the programs, and he and a young female colleague on the staff performed a scene from Thornton Wilder's *Our Town*—the scene with George and Emily as young teenagers. This was a special treat for the audience because they were actually seeing Caucasian actors playing Caucasian characters, unlike the rest of us who were Japanese pretending to be Caucasians.

Though it was ironic, we did this out of necessity. There were no plays about Japanese Americans, much less works written by Nisei Americans. That came later, after the war.

But I don't think the audience minded the arrangement. For most, it was like going to see Hollywood movies, where one rarely saw a Japanese character. Of course, during wartime, when Hollywood was fighting the "Japs," there were many Japanese characters—all portrayed by Chinese and Koreans.

The Little Theater came to an abrupt end with the institution of the loyalty registration order in early February 1943, when politics displaced art, when division, distrust, even enmity among the members— all caused by the infamous order—effectively killed off any creative energy within the group. The last performances were in January, and by mid-February the Little Theater at Tule Lake was history.

Starting from Loomis . . . Again

I renounced my American citizenship at Tule Lake, and I feel that was the dumbest thing I ever did in my life. It was a terrible mistake for which I have paid dearly.

I had opposed the registration in protest against the many injustices I had suffered—not just the incarceration but all the racist abuses I had taken as a child and as a young man, all the times I had been called a "Jap."

For my action, or inaction, I was later segregated from the rest of the camp population. Me, a kid from Loomis, segregated in a maximum security prison for "disloyal" Americans. I didn't know what my fate would be; I was hoping that nothing drastic would happen.

I just wanted to be who I was—a Japanese American, an American of Japanese descent, an American citizen. Since they would not release me, I had no choice but to sit out the war in camp.

Obviously, I was not pro-Japan, even if I could read and write Japanese; I was, in fact, more advanced in the Japanese language than those hastily trained at the military language school. With my language skill, I realize now that I could have been very useful to my country. I would have been trained at the military language school and would have served in the Military Intelligence Service, where

DOI: 10.5876/9781607322542.c13

many Kibei* and Nisei served with honor. If only the country had been more fair and trusting.

But renunciation was another thing. First the US Congress passed a law making it easier for American citizens to renounce their citizenship. When I first heard about the law, I felt it was only for pro-Japan fanatics, certainly not for me. I had no real desire to go to Japan, so I tried not to concern myself with it. But unknowingly, I was swept into the clamor, and I succumbed to the pressure—both outside and within my family.

In the year after the loyalty questionnaire, Tule Lake became an increasingly tense, hostile, and dangerous place. Around 8,000 people from other camps who had also either refused to answer or answered no to the loyalty questionnaire were brought to Tule Lake; soon, talk of renunciation was in the air.

Pro-Japan factions were pressuring others; some urged me to join their group, the Hoshi Dan, and told me that for my own sake I must renounce my US citizenship. Although I refused to join them, I was also afraid of defying them. The atmosphere in camp was menacing— there were stealing and beatings and killings. It was dangerous to even speak English during this time because we would be called "White Japs." I grew increasingly afraid that I might become a marked man if I didn't follow the crowd.

In Block 40, where we lived, there was also agitation for repatriation, which often broke out in open hostilities. People questioned each other about where they stood on the subject. As I was secretary to the block manager, many people came to me asking for help in acquiring and filling out the repatriation forms. I listened to their questions and fears, and they only deepened my own.

---

* Kibei is a term that describes a Japanese American born in the US who returned to the US after living in Japan.

I was influenced by a family friend whose wife and children were in Japan. He was planning to join them after the war, so it was natural for him to be pro-Japan. He came every day to visit Mother and to give us counsel, urging us to renounce. I tried not to listen to him, but I guess he was an influence—he was one of the few older male figures I could talk to. Though in my heart I didn't agree with him, I didn't want to defy him either.

My brother, who worked with some of the pro-Japan fanatics in the mess hall and came under their sway, forced the issue one day: "Are we American or are we Japanese? Let's make it clear." And I gave in.

In December 1944 I sent a letter requesting renunciation of citizenship for myself and my siblings. At the hearing in February 1945, I was afraid. I remember barely being able to speak. I had not talked with a Caucasian in over three years. Because of what had happened to us, I was filled with fear and distrust and resentment. We knew what questions would be asked from previous interviews; I just wanted to get it over with.

The renunciation was approved on March 22, 1945. I admit there was a brief feeling of relief once the ordeal was over. My mother was glad that, whatever might happen to us from then on, we would at least be together and be safe from the dangers inside and outside the camp. I also believed by that point that I was not wanted in America—my government had made that quite clear.

But renunciation was totally unnecessary. I realized that in the months to come, and I still believe it to this day. We had already made our protest known by not registering. Giving up our citizenship was stupid and redundant. Since I did not possess Japanese or any other citizenship, I essentially became a person without a country. My official status, in fact, became "Native American Alien"—what a preposterous predicament!

I think that after several years of incarceration I had lost all initiative to do anything new or daring on my own; I was barely hanging on, sticking to the familiar daily routine of camp life in fear that I would fall apart. Playing baseball with others like myself helped while we were involved in the game, but when the game ended it was back to bleak, numb reality. I guess this is what it is like to be incarcerated except that, in my case, my future was a big unknown—the war between the United States and Japan was still going on.

Still, I was lazy; I didn't want to think; I didn't want to confront the problem and make a decision, put my foot down, and assert my real feelings. Without Father there to guide us, I had a responsibility, and I know now that I should have stood up to my younger brother. Honestly, I never relished being the *chonan*, the firstborn son, not since we were kids. My brother, who was always tough, a class leader if not a bully, liked to be in control; by the time we were sharecropping the farm, he was doing the heavy work. In addition, like his father, he always planned several days ahead so he was on top of things. So I let him be the chonan, and our roles were reversed. I was happy with that until renunciation—when he forced the issue of our citizenship and I felt that I gave in to his power play. I think I thought all of it would somehow go away. For my refusal to face reality, I would pay dearly.

Perhaps I should not be too hard on myself? Perhaps I was the victim? I feel I have paid many times over for the position I took at Tule Lake. Certainly, you don't go around telling people you spent time at Tule Lake and gave up your citizenship during the war. You try to push that back somewhere and not think about it; you try to block out that part of your life, but you have to live with it. You try to find a safe niche in society and hope no one will pry into your past. Living under such pressure, it's inevitable that there should be doubts and questions about your actions, as well as feelings of guilt. Were my actions wrong or bad? What kind of man did this make me? I guess I couldn't help but live with these feelings as the years went on and I grew older.

Swimming in the American

Swimming was our principal form of recreation in the summer. As kids, we could not go swimming unless the temperature hit 90 degrees or above—so we put the thermometer out in the sun, sometimes shaking it impatiently, and barely waited until it reached 90. Then we rushed off with our swimming trunks to our favorite swimming hole in the American River, about four miles away. How exciting it was, going to the river, standing in the back of the pickup truck. I learned to swim the summer I was eleven and in the process nearly drowned.

After three Sundays of practice, I thought I was ready to do the crawl stroke across the river, a distance of about ten yards; others were doing the dog paddle. I had learned the stroke from an older Nisei boy, Hal, who was visiting from Sacramento. He called it the "Australian crawl," a rather showy style with elaborate arm movements. I hadn't learned to breathe properly, so I held my breath as I made the plunge. I was doing fine for five or six strokes, then for some reason I stopped; maybe I needed air or thought I had made the crossing. I hadn't. I was vertical, and my eyes were full of water. I couldn't touch bottom. I panicked and cried for help. Hal, who was watching me, tossed me an inflated tire tube, but I was blinded and couldn't see, so he dived in and pulled me to shore. It was a scare I never forgot. It was my first real challenge

DOI: 10.5876/9781607322542.c14

in life and my first failure; I felt foolish, but mercifully no one faulted me for trying. Recently, I related the incident to Hal's widow, who was completely unaware of it. She and I shared a moment, remembering Hal, appreciating the kind, selfless person he was.

Father, who was downstream and had observed the entire scene, said later, "I was waiting to pull you out when you came downstream." I couldn't understand his remark; I thought it was callous considering that I had nearly drowned. But Father was a strong, confident swimmer; his dives from a high boulder were spectacular.

Mother, too, was a fair swimmer, with rather busy sidestrokes. She had grown up near a river, where she and her brother used to swim in the summer. In 1989, six years after Mother's death, my wife and I visited my uncle and aunt in Wakayama. Uncle hired a taxi, and we drove about an hour to the old homesite. Mother always said she came from deep in the *inaka* (country). It was rural all right, but beautiful. I wish I could have convinced Mother of that. To the north was a forest of trees, and to the west on a hill was where my grandfather had worked his crops. The land had been sold after my grandmother's death, and the house was gone, but down to the south was the river where my uncle and mother had played in the summers. "I can still picture us swimming in the river," my uncle said, recalling the happy days of their childhood.

After coming out of the concentration camp in early 1946, I spent 100 days at a labor camp cutting asparagus. We didn't work all of the 100 days, only when the weather got warm and the "grass" began to sprout. But when we did work, it was absolutely backbreaking. I have never worked that hard since. Still, we were free, free to come and go; after over three years of confinement, there was no feeling like it.

Besides, we were paid well for our work. My brother, I, and three others were a team of five. When the season was over, we each walked out with a check for $1,000. This was after deducting our board, taxi fares to town, recreation costs—games of pool and movies—and maybe a gift for the lady cook who worked at the labor camp, a very important person for workers.

After the asparagus season, we returned to Loomis, where Mother was sharing a cabin with two other families. That summer we worked picking plums for the owner of the ranch and cabin.

One Sunday on our day off my brother and I, along with a few other young Nisei, went to cool off once again in the American River. The river was cold and fast-moving, treacherous as ever, I thought. I remembered my near-drowning experience, so I was a little nervous. We looked for a cove for safe wading and swimming.

My brother and I were the only ones who could swim. Others were using inflated pillowcases as floats, which was not the safest thing to do, as we learned when one of the floats deflated and the girl using it cried out for help.

My brother was out of the water. I was the only one nearby, so I reached out and the girl grabbed my hand, then wrapped her arms around me. Thus entangled, we went straight down into the American.

As we descended, I remember saying to myself, "Here we go." I was completely relaxed, resigned to whatever was going to happen as we sank deeper beneath the river's surface. Strangely, it was an exhilarating feeling, like we were entering a totally new realm. Like Urashima Taro, the fisherman in the Japanese folktale, we were in a watery kingdom inhabited by mermaids.

We soon hit bottom feet-first and, miraculously, bounded right up. It was unbelievable; only then did I realize that we weren't going to drown.

SWIMMING IN THE AMERICAN

Holding my companion, I struggled to get back to shore. It was rather messy, especially compared to the miracle of the previous moment. When the girl later thanked me for saving her life, I was embarrassed. I didn't feel heroic at all. I was just thankful that we were still alive.

Tuberculosis in Our Family

Tuberculosis was the bane of our family. I believe the disease was ever present in our household. My youngest sister succumbed to tuberculosis meningitis at age three-and-a-half, when I was a freshman at Placer Union High School. My other sister was diagnosed with TB after she came out of camp, but she was able to overcome it even after several relapses. She was fortunate that new medicines were available after World War II.

In the fall of 1939 my parents sent me to Los Angeles, where I worked as a houseboy and attended Dorsey High School, graduating in June 1940. I believe that is what saved my life—the nine months I was away from home and away from being exposed to Father's tuberculosis. Fortunately, I have had a lifetime free of major illnesses, though my annual chest X-rays always show scar tissue, evidence of childhood TB.

In 1933, when Father was hospitalized for pleurisy, we were told that the store was being torn down to make way for a new highway. Mother was still recovering from giving birth to our baby sister. We had no place to go. Fortunately for us, though, a kind family offered to take us in, and we moved into their small outbuilding where Father was able to recuperate from his illness.

DOI: 10.5876/9781607322542:c15

When plowing season came, Father volunteered to do the plowing. Mother knew he wasn't fully recovered. "Are you sure you're well enough to do the work?" she asked him. "Don't worry, I'm all right," he said. He was determined to do the hard work; he felt obligated to the family who had taken us in, and this was his way to repay their kindness. So he worked every day. It was hard work following the horse, guiding the plow, walking over rough terrain hour after hour. When he slept at night, thoroughly exhausted, Mother noticed a wheezing sound to his breathing that she knew wasn't normal. She pleaded with him to stop working, but Father was a stubborn man; he would work until he finished the job—plowing the entire twenty acres of the ranch. Mother knew that was the beginning of the disease that would ravage his lungs and be the source of anguish for our family.

What was most difficult was that my parents wouldn't admit that Father had tuberculosis, not to us children and certainly not to anyone outside the family. I admit that I was an accomplice in this because I always knew, even though my parents might have thought I didn't. I was a perceptive kid; I knew all their secrets.

His illness must have been common knowledge in the community because fewer and fewer people seemed to be coming to shop at the store. Then one day a Caucasian woman came in, unannounced. She was a quiet, kindly woman, like a Japanese *obasan*, or auntie, I thought. She introduced herself as a social worker.

She said she wanted to ask a few things about our family, such as who comprised the household. I interpreted for Mother. Then she asked where Father was, and Mother replied that he was away on business. "Is there anything troubling your family?" she asked, and I looked at Mother who shook her head. I knew she was in denial, and I told the lady there was nothing troubling us. She looked as though she didn't believe us. There was an awkward moment; though I was only inter-preting for Mother, I felt I was an accomplice in the deceit. The woman got up and thanked us for the time. Mother and I were relieved. But before leaving, she said that if we had any problems to call her, and she left us her card. Mother and I were shocked to learn that she was from the county health department.

That is when Mother finally told me that Father had TB. "But we must not tell anyone," she added. Though I already knew, it was shock-ing to hear her say it. TB was such a dreaded disease; TB was conta-gious. When people admitted to suffering from it, they were sent to a sanatorium, isolated, separate, away from family and other people. The treatment was usually bedrest, sometimes a collapsed lung. Very few recovered; it was a life in a bathrobe, a slow, lonely death.

Years later, I wondered what would have happened if we hadn't perpetrated the lie and told the woman the truth—that there was an active case of TB in the family. The consequences would have been too much to bear. Not only would I have betrayed my parents, but what would have happened to our family? Father would have been sent away, and what would we have done? I think Mother would have been able to run the store. I might have had to quit school or stay home to help. But would there have been any customers? I'm sure my parents consid-ered all these consequences. So Father sacrificed his health for the sake of the family, but at the same time he was exposing us and others to his TB—and my two sisters became victims.

Soon, Father stopped making his rounds to peddle fish and deliver groceries, and customers stopped coming to the store entirely. There was no point in continuing the business. He stopped running the store in 1939, the summer before I left for Los Angeles. He found a ranch to sharecrop in a neighboring town; the twenty-acre ranch was small enough that he wouldn't have to do much physical labor.

Mother tried to protect us children by sterilizing everything Father used—his clothing, bedding, and eating utensils were kept separate from the rest of the family. Father, too, kept at a distance, only super-vising as Mother did the routine work. My brother tended to the heavy work after school and on weekends. In the summer when school was out, I returned home and joined the family in harvesting the fruit. Everything seemed to be working well. The ranch owner was satisfied that the necessary work was being done.

Then one day Father coughed up blood. This so alarmed my parents that they contacted the health department, and he was soon admitted to Weimar Sanatorium. That was in early 1941.

The sanatorium was about fifteen miles from our home. Mother made frequent visits, and my brother, sister, and I took turns going with her on a Greyhound bus. At first, Father was concerned about us, asking how we were doing on the ranch. We assured him that everything was fine—the boss wasn't complaining—so he shouldn't worry. In time he stopped asking; he looked more relaxed, perhaps resigned, as he adjusted to his confinement.

Father remained at Weimar Sanatorium when we left for camp in April 1942. About ten days before we left for camp, we went to say goodbye to Father. Fortunately, we still had the sedan, so all four of us went to see him. It was a sad visit for all of us. I think Father said some-thing like "Who knows when we'll see each other again. Stay well." In my mind I've kept the image of him standing in his bathrobe, wav-ing to us, lonely, as we drove away. We would not see him again until March 1946 when we were released from camp.

Although we had adjusted to life without him, we missed him. We missed him during the traumatic days before leaving for camp, when we had to settle our affairs hurriedly and pack to leave for an unknown place and an uncertain future. We missed his reassuring presence. And we missed him when we had to face the registration and loyalty questions.

Our only contact with Father during those years was through letters. An inveterate letter writer, he wrote more often than we did. When the registration order came, it would have been so much easier if Father had been there to make the crucial decisions. I don't know what position he would have taken, but he would have made the decision and we would have either followed it or opposed it.

When we informed him of our decision to oppose the registration, all he wrote was, "If that's your decision, I won't say anything." But I had a feeling that he did have something to say and didn't. Years later, I wondered if we had put him in a difficult and awkward position. His family was in a camp for "disloyal Americans," and he was at the mercy of American doctors and nurses. He never complained, though, so I never knew.

After we came out of camp, we tried to visit Father whenever we could. Our reunion was both happy and awkward—happy because it was our first meeting in three-and-a-half years and awkward because we didn't know how to handle our emotions. So much time had passed, and so much had happened. All our feelings were expressed in our handshakes. I believe my father said, "I'm glad you're back. It's been a long time. It's good to see all of you."

Once, after we had settled on a ranch nearby, Father came out for a week. Mother would sometimes say she was widowed at forty when Father first showed signs of TB, that their marriage had only lasted about twenty years. But that week together again was a good time for all of us, almost normal. I remember one night my brother and I went out to see a movie to give our parents time to themselves. We knew their time together was brief and precious.

In the fall of 1947, after the grape harvest, we decided to move to Los Angeles. I would attend school, my brother would find work in the city, and Mother would come with us. When we told Father, he looked pained but said nothing. My sister survived the war years and, after coming out of camp in March 1946, she worked as a live-in maid for a family in San Francisco. We were in the Lodi labor camp picking grapes when we heard that she had TB and was being sent to Weimar Sanatorium. After we left for Los Angeles, she would be the only one near our father.

Father spent the balance of his life confined at Weimar while we were free, busy living our lives, looking to the future with new hope. Father, in contrast, had no such outlook. His days were the same, numbered, bleak. It must have been a lonely, frustrating life, especially since Father had been such an active man before his illness.

Father died in 1951 while I was attending UCLA. Mother, my brother, and I came up from Los Angeles to arrange for the funeral. My sister was still at Weimar Sanatorium and didn't attend the service. A prominent community leader who volunteered to chair the service lauded Father's contribution to the community: how as a storekeeper he had offered credit to people during the Depression when they had no money to pay cash; how he had worked tirelessly to organize the Mutual Benefit Society, a community cooperative to pay for people's funeral expenses; and how he worked to build the Japanese-language school in Loomis. From my perspective, my father's life was very brief—only sixty-three years—but he accomplished much in that short time. That day, hearing his story told, I was never so proud of my father.

Summer Job at Mount Baldy

While I was in college in Los Angeles after the war, I never thought to plan ahead for a summer job while school was still in session. Does this mean I was so immersed in my studies that I could not look ahead to summer, when classes were over? I doubt that that was the case, but, whatever the reason, only after final exams were completed would I head to the employment office. By then, all the desirable jobs were gone. Only jobs no one wanted were left—unpleasant, low-paying jobs or those that were in some remote area, far from the city. But I had to work; back in my day, most of us had to pay our own way through school if we wanted to go to college.

Once, in desperation, I went to a Chinese employment agency in Los Angeles's Little Tokyo, and the agent offered me what he called a "good job" as a dishwasher at a resort in Mount Baldy.

"But where is that?" I asked.

"About twenty miles from here in the mountains."

"How would I get there?"

"Take the Greyhound bus to Upland, and the boss will come after you there."

DOI: 10.5876/9781607322542.c16

I took the job. I had no other choice. The summer was half over, and I desperately needed to make money for the fall semester. On the bus was another Asian man, older than I. I wondered if he was going to Upland too. He was.

At the Greyhound depot we were met by the boss, a Caucasian, who seemed happy to see us. After all, he was filling two positions at once—the cook and the dishwasher—and we had arrived. There were Kim, the cook, who to me would always be Kim-san; the boss (I have forgotten his name, if I ever knew it); and myself.

After a five- or six-mile drive over a steep, winding road, we were at the resort. It was a popular ski resort in the winter, but in the middle of summer it seemed almost deserted. The boss showed us our quarters—we were each assigned a separate cabin that was simply furnished with a double bed, a dresser, a closet, and a separate bathroom. There was a single chair and no desk or table. If the cabin needed to accommodate a couple, where was the other chair? I wondered. Or would one person sit in the other's lap?

Kim-san was very professional-looking in his chef's cap, white jacket, and wraparound apron. No one was allowed in the cooking area, not even the boss. That was Kim-san's domain. He took great pains in planning the menu for each day, although much of his cooking was devoted to short orders. He fixed an elaborate breakfast for me every morning. I swear he used half a dozen eggs for my scrambled eggs. "Boss won't know the difference," he would say. Kim-san himself subsisted on rice gruel, which he ate all day long. It was different from the *ochazuke*, or hot tea over cold rice, I was accustomed to. His consisted of cold water over cold rice. I believe he also ate *kim chee* (spicy pickled vegetables), which he made. He never offered it to me. "Only Koreans eat this food," he said, implying that I wasn't Korean.

"You Japanese?" he asked me one day. When I told him I was, he said, "I don't like Japanese. When I see one, I take him, pow!" swinging his closed fist, luckily not at me but at some hateful but imaginary

Japanese. Is he a madman? I wondered. But soon he said, "You okay," putting me at ease.

The resort had a few short-order customers during the day, and there were eight or ten diners every evening. My job as a dishwasher was rather easy. I think I spent more time washing the pots and pans Kim-san used and piled up. For the little cooking he does, he sure goes through a lot of utensils, I thought. But I had quite a bit of downtime. Once, to look busy, I grabbed a broom, intending to sweep the outside porch, but Kim-san stopped me. "You were hired as a dishwasher, nothing else," he said and took the broom from me.

After the lunch dishes were done, I had free time from around 2:00 to 5:00 p.m. Kim-san took a nap every day, but I didn't need one. I read the newspaper very thoroughly, including all the ads. I wished I had taken a book to read, but I hadn't; the reception on my transistor radio wasn't good at that elevation; I tried writing a few letters but soon realized that I didn't have much to write about. If I caught the mailman at the right time, I could ride with him to Upland, but what would I do there? Besides, I would have had to trudge back up the mountain, an arduous task.

I decided to go hiking and explore the area (I think it was in the San Gabriel Mountains). On my first hike I was gone for over two hours, enjoying being among the trees and fascinated with the different flora I was seeing, when I suddenly realized that I had strayed from the path. I have to get out before dark, I thought. It was summer, and there was plenty of time before darkness fell. Just don't panic, I told myself. I wandered around, probably going in circles, trying to find my way. I had climbed to get where I was, so logically I should now be descending, I thought. While trying to find a way down, quite by accident I hit upon a trail, which I took. What a close call that was. But since I was back on time for work, no one was aware of my scary misadventure. I didn't go hiking after that but tried to find other ways to spend my time, like whittling—a new activity—and I managed to carve a few nondescript objects. But boredom became a problem.

After exactly a month, our stay at Mount Baldy was over, none too soon for me. After paying Kim-san and me, the boss drove us down to Upland, where we boarded the Greyhound bus back to Los Angeles. On the bus, I told Kim-san how much I had enjoyed working with him, even though it was only for a month. Kim-san said, "I like you even though you are Japanese." He added, "I want to fix you up with a nice Korean girl."

"Fine with me," I said. When we parted at the Greyhound depot at 7th and Main, I didn't think I would see Kim-san again, but a few weeks later I got a call. The voice, though drunk, was familiar. It was Kim-san calling from a bar on Skid Row. "Come on down here. I want to buy you lunch," he said. As directed, I went downtown to Jack's Place on 5th Street. Kim-san waved me in. He was quite drunk. This was surprising to me because he had been totally sober during the time we were at Mount Baldy.

"You like a beer?" he asked.

"No," I said. "Coffee?"

"Coffee for the boy, and some pig knuckles, too," he yelled to someone in the back.

"You like pig knuckles?"

"I never had them."

"You got to try them."

I sat in a booth where I was served a plate with three pig knuckles. I picked one up and started to gnaw on it. There was a slightly sour taste of what was mostly bone and gristle. I did the best I could with them while Kim-san had another beer at the bar. I felt out of place and decided to leave; I got up to thank Kim-san.

"You going already?"

"Yeah, thanks for lunch."

"You're welcome. Remember, I'm gonna find you a nice Korean girl," he said.

"That's fine," I said and left.

That was the last I saw of Kim-san. Needless to say, the nice Korean girl never materialized.

Nisei Experimental Group and Later

I happened to meet Hiro Okubo one day at the main library in Los Angeles, where I was working as a page in the Literature Department. This was during my college days. We had been classmates in the advanced Japanese class at the Tule Lake camp. That was enough to start a conversation. We discovered that we shared an interest in theater. Hiro was taking an acting class in the evenings at Los Angeles City College (LACC), where I was also enrolled (though I was a day student in the English department). After our first meeting, we met often. In time, we decided to form a theater group.

We put a notice in the *Rafu Shimpo*, the Japanese American community paper in Los Angeles. Among the half-dozen interested people who responded was Albert Saijo, a writer who had recently gained notoriety in the community for his critical review of Toshio Mori's seminal book *Yokohama, California*. Albert served as adviser to the group. He wasn't particularly interested in acting, as most of us were. He suggested the name "Nisei Experimental Group," which we adopted; thus, the first postwar Japanese American theater group was started in 1948.

Through the kindness of Father Lavery, we met weekly at the Maryknoll Church. The first order of business was to learn the rudiments of acting. Hiro, as the group's leader, shared what he was learning

DOI: 10.5876/9781607322542:c17

in his acting class at LACC. After months of dull routines, we started to work on short scenes from Broadway plays until we felt comfortable enough to perform in front of an audience. But there were no plays suitable for our group. We certainly didn't want to do Broadway shows. So I decided to write a play. After reading a book on playwriting, I wrote *Plums Can Wait*, our first production.

The one-act play was based in part on an incident that occurred soon after we came out of camp. In the play, two brothers and their mother are hired as laborers on a plum ranch when one day, out of the blue, the boss's wife accuses them of malingering. Angered by the accusation, they tell her they are quitting. It is the middle of the picking season, and the plums are heavy on the trees. The boss comes to apologize for his wife and tries to talk them out of leaving; he offers them a five-cent-an-hour raise. Now, the conflict is between the brothers. The older, conscientious and long-suffering like his late father, feels they should stay; but the younger, fiery and angry, says he's through taking abuse and starts to leave, only to be stopped by their mother, who pleads with him not to break up the family.

The play ran about forty minutes, so to fill out the program we had two performances, each with a different cast and director. One performance was directed by Hiro, who added some Japanese touches— the use of wooden clappers to open and close the play and *shakuhachi* (bamboo flute) music to heighten certain scenes. The second, more straightforward performance was directed by Ted Samuel, a recent graduate of the Pasadena Playhouse, who also played Mr. White, the boss. We had met Ted when he was performing in *Ghost Sonata* at the Orchard Gables Theater in Hollywood. He offered to help with our first production. Ted and I became lifelong friends. After we both moved to San Francisco, Ted directed my later plays, all performed by the Center Players in the late 1970s and early 1980s.

The audience at our first production in the second-floor conference room of the old Miyako Hotel in Los Angeles was small. I think most

Japanese were too busy reestablishing themselves after the lost years in camp to attend theatrical productions. But among the ten to fifteen people was Molly (Mary) Oyama, an influential Nisei newspaper columnist who became our most ardent patron. In fact, she informed Marlon Brando about the production. Brando, who was making his first film, *The Men*, couldn't come but sent regrets through an Israeli friend. Later, when Molly hosted a party to celebrate the success of our first production, Marlon Brando and his friend showed up. So we had the rare privilege of socializing with the most exciting American actor of the day.

Hiro had been exposed to classical Japanese tradition through his sister, an accomplished classical Japanese dancer, and his father, a perennial stagehand for the Kabuki and other traditional shows presented in Little Tokyo (Japantown). So it was inevitable that our next production would be a series of Kyogen plays, or short, comic interludes for Noh plays.

Though the plays were translated into English, they required a certain stylized form of acting that took several months to master. After six months we were ready to present our second production—a series of four Kyogen comedies, again in the Miyako Hotel conference room. With simple suggestive sets and fairly authentic costumes and props, we presented our version, or, I should say, Hiro Okubo's interpretation, of the classical plays. But the humor in the plays carried the day. Many in the audience called the plays "delightful."

In the audience was Jobo Nakamura, a writer for San Francisco's *Hokubei Mainichi*, who happened to be in Los Angeles during the time of the production. He was impressed with our show and wondered if we did other plays. When we told him about *Plums Can Wait*, he thought we should perform it along with the Kyogen plays in the Bay Area. He would arrange it.

So a few months later, I believe in early 1950, ten or eleven of us traveled by Greyhound bus to San Francisco. We were sponsored by the Buchanan YMCA and the San Francisco chapter of the Japanese American Citizens League. We did two performances of *Plums Can Wait* and the Kyogen plays, one in San Francisco and one at the Berkeley Little Theatre. I think we made a good impression; we were reviewed favorably by the critics from both the *San Francisco Chronicle* and the *Oakland Tribune*. But sadly, our greatest triumph turned out to be our last hurrah because the group disbanded soon after our trip. I never understood why we broke up.

I came to UC Berkeley in September 1952. Though I was a graduate student in art history, a new major for me, I also took a course in playwriting for which I wrote my second play, *Laughter and False Teeth*. The long one-act tragicomedy was set in a concentration camp for Japanese Americans during World War II. The play had a studio production with a large cast made up of Nisei students, none of whom had acted before. The part of the MP, of course, was played by a Caucasian student. The play was well received by the campus audience, I felt.

One day I attended a concert reading of a classical Greek play and was moved and impressed with the work of the faculty director and the performers, who were mainly older former students. So I auditioned for a part in Shakespeare's *The Tempest* and was cast as Caliban; later, I read the part of Bosola in Webster's *The Duchess of Malfi*. I also played Balthazar, one of the three kings in *Nativity Cycle*, which was a full production—complete with music, costumes, and stage horses for the kings. As a result of my activities in the theater department, I was elected to the Mask and Dagger Society, an unexpected honor.

Meanwhile, my master's thesis, which was supposed to be a study of Buddhist art, remained idle and incomplete. My lame excuse to myself was that my adviser was in Europe on a year's sabbatical. It was easy to ignore it when I had too many fun things like acting that I wanted to do. However, years later I returned to campus and completed work for a master's degree in library science.

Though acting became a part-time activity after graduate school, I managed to appear in several plays at the Asian American Theater Company in San Francisco in the late 1970s. My most notable stage work was with the late actress Nobu McCarthy in Philip Kan Gotanda's *The Wash* at the Eureka Theatre in San Francisco.

I had an agent who would call me about auditions, but it was often difficult to take time away from my job and I probably missed out on some parts. I did appear in a few TV commercials and "industrials" (films such as employee training videos) and in such films as *Black Rain*, *Dark Circle*, and *Hito Hata—Raise the Banner*, the first Asian American feature film. I was also fortunate to work in award-winning filmmaker Emiko Omori's *Hot Summer Winds* and *Rabbit in the Moon*. I am proudest of my most recent film work with Tim Yamamura in *The Virtues of Corned Beef Hash*, a short, independent film by Kerwin Berk.

I did better as a playwright, especially through my association with the Center Players, a theater group formed expressly to perform my plays. The group was responsible for the 1975 revival of *Plums Can Wait* and *Laughter and False Teeth*, and I was inspired to write three new plays—*Blessed Be*, *A Window for Aya*, and *The Betrayed*—all produced in the late 1970s by the Center Players and directed by my friend Ted Samuel. *The Betrayed* enjoyed a revival in 2010 by the Grateful Crane Ensemble, my son Soji's theater company in Los Angeles, and has had performances at the Japanese American National Museum in Los Angeles, the Orange County Buddhist Church, and the Torrance Cultural Arts Center.

I have been called a "pioneer" Japanese American writer, playwright, and actor. I suppose it's meant as a compliment for having paved the way for others to follow. I should be gracious and accept it as such, but I can't. I feel ambivalent about the accolade. First, it makes me seem ancient, an annoyance to someone as old as I am who is still active. In fact, I have to reject such thoughts so I can stay active. Second, there is a matter of ego, so crucial in the creative process. By being called a "pioneer," I sense a feeling of dismissal or even rejection, which really raises my hackles. I would prefer to be judged on my work, past and present; that would be easier to accept, no matter how critical. Now, all this is probably just in my head, but that's how it is.

Career as a Librarian

Librarianship was not my first choice as a career, but in the 1960s there was a shortage of librarians and the field was opening up to males and minorities, so I took what was available. I had worked for five years as translator/interpreter, editor, and English-language secretary for the Buddhist headquarters. Though satisfying, the job did not pay enough to support a family that included a wife and three young boys, so I was looking for other job opportunities. I thought of teaching high school English, but that opportunity was closed to minorities. I took the Federal Civil Service exams, did well, even had interviews, but no job was forthcoming. My dream was to work for the government in the Foreign Service, but that was absurd considering my No-No Boy history.

Then I had a chance meeting with a fellow parent at Frederic Burk Elementary School. Our oldest boy had been accepted to this prestigious demonstration school of San Francisco State College because the school was trying to diversify its students. In my conversation with the parent, the assistant city librarian of the San Francisco Public Library, the subject of the Japanese language came up. I mentioned that I had a BA in Asian languages from UCLA, with an emphasis in Japanese. "How about working for the library? We could use a Japanese-speaking librarian," he said.

DOI: 10.5876/9781607322542:c18

So I enrolled at the library school at UC Berkeley and commuted by car from San Francisco for two semesters. I attained a master's degree in library science, which qualified me to work as a professional librarian. That was a difficult year. We lived on funds borrowed from family members, a small government loan, and income from occasional temporary jobs I could fit into my schedule. I remember working as a temporary clerk at the Post Office during Christmas vacation.

Though I was promised a job, I was interviewed on campus by a panel from the San Francisco Public Library, headed by City Librarian William Holman. Despite its large collection, the San Francisco Public Library had a miserable reputation when Holman took over as city librarian. He knew the staff was substandard; many of the librarians had come up through the ranks and were untrained. He set a policy to hire graduates of library schools and recruited young women, preferably attractive ones, and more men and minorities. When I was hired, I was one of two Asians on the staff. The new hires brought youth, energy, diversity, and a new standard of service that put the San Francisco Public Library well on the way to becoming a dynamic, modern library.

I am proud that I was once one of the "Young Turks" who turned the library around. At first, as required, the men wore coats and neckties, then the ties became more colorful and psychedelic in keeping with the times—the hippie era in San Francisco—and disappeared entirely when Levi jeans were in fashion. The women also took to wearing pants instead of dresses. The staid old San Francisco Public Library was now "hip" and contemporary.

I was hired to work in the library's Literature Department, starting in June 1966. Apparently, I had made a strong impression because one of the panelists told me later that Holman had commented that I had the best literature background of all the applicants he had interviewed. That was nice to hear. A few years later, when Holman left the system, his last words to me were, "You're an asset to the library and to the citizens of San Francisco." I had never heard such praise before, and from a man for whom I had great respect. Going home on the bus, I remember saying to myself, "I feel like I've been knighted."

In addition to the general reference work in literature, we were assigned certain areas of specialization. Mine was in the foreign language section. I selected books and materials in Spanish, Japanese, and Gaelic. I had studied Spanish in college and Japanese had been my major, but Gaelic? This was a completely foreign language to me, but I soon learned that to function as a librarian, one does not necessarily need to know the language but must be familiar with the writers and their works. There is a body of literature in Gaelic, and our collection was small and selective. I'm happy that I added a few books to it. Spanish books and materials were mostly confined to the literature of the "New World." I became familiar with many Spanish writers, some of whom were major figures in world literature.

My primary interest, however, was in Japanese-language books and materials. When I started in 1966, there must have been fewer than ten books in Japanese in the library. I tried to build a collection that would be of most interest to readers—works by contemporary writers, best-sellers in Japan, and classics of the modern period. Within a few years the collection had grown quickly, and it was moved to the Western Addition Branch Library, where it would be more accessible to patrons who read Japanese.

Today, the library holds about 17,500 Japanese-language materials and about 1,500 Japanese- and Japanese American–related books in English; the current city librarian has called it "the only collection of its kind in America." I am also pleased and honored that the San Francisco Library Commission has recognized me for developing the Japanese collection. The plaque with the inscription is on display at the Western Addition Branch Library.

Though it was relatively brief, a few months short of twenty years, I really enjoyed my career as a librarian. In fact, I looked forward to going to work every morning. I became something of an expert on modern Japanese literature. With the cooperation of the Japanese Consulate, I did an exhibit on the subject at the main library. I was also invited to lecture on the topic at a library conference held at the University of San Francisco.

Every question posed by a patron was a challenge. In those pre-computer days, we would hunt for the information in books. It was my habit to run my fingers across and down the page as I looked for the information—a patron once asked me if I read with my fingers.

I did encounter some racism on the job. That was hard to take. One patron used the term *Jap* in my presence. I remember taking a moment, wondering what to do. I decided I couldn't let it pass, so I stood up to the perpetrator and made him apologize.

But most patrons were grateful for the service we provided. Some wrote letters of commendation for my personnel file. Once, after I had served a patron, he slapped a five-dollar bill into my hand.

I had changed my major three times in college, so I had a lot of loose information in my head that was helpful in handling reference questions, especially over the telephone when speed was important. My experience as an actor and writer also helped.

At the monthly staff meetings, I tried to make my oral report as interesting as I could. I thought librarians took themselves and their work too seriously. I guess I was trying to change that, to liven up the dull meetings. Soon I had a reputation for giving interesting reports, and I could get up and say anything and the librarians would laugh. As an example of the travails of a branch librarian, I reported that one day I went into the staff room and caught somebody escaping out one of the library windows—one leg was out the window, but the other leg was still in the room. I was so dumbfounded at this sight that I let the culprit get away!

But when my reports became too entertaining, almost a comedy routine, my supervisor warned me that they had too much "levity," which put a stop to that.

Some supervisors or heads of departments or branches would agonize for days writing their monthly reports, a task that took me less than ten minutes. I often wondered how they ever got hired, much less promoted.

During my career as a librarian, I was transferred to work in the Science and Documents Department. I knew little or nothing about science, and it was a challenge to learn the subjects quickly so I could function as a librarian. The San Francisco Public Library is also a repository for federal, state, and local documents. Working with the documents was educational—I became quite familiar with the workings of our government. So the job made me grow in some ways, too.

I was manager of several different branches in the city—the Western Addition, North Beach, and Parkside Branches. I was also assigned to the Excelsior Branch. These assignments gave me a chance to learn about the different neighborhoods in the city. My favorite was the North Beach Branch, which served so many diverse neighborhoods: North Beach, of course; Chinatown; and Fishermen's Wharf.

Most of all, what was best about being a librarian was simply being surrounded by so many books, all that knowledge, all day, every day. That and being free to pursue my other interests, like acting and writing, after work. I know that many people think libraries can be boring places, but I can attest: working in one can be a lot of fun.

Barracuda and Other Fish

(FOR SADAKO)

I developed a love for fish of all kinds growing up in a fish market. I still remember watching my father, an ex-fisherman, cutting the fish deftly with his large, sword-like knives. Over the years, I have eaten so many of them, big and small, that I have a good knowledge of fish, especially their anatomy.

Tuna and sea bass are usually served raw as sashimi, but with the introduction of sushi to American cuisine, they are better known as essential ingredients for nigirizushi. However, my mother, who often had access to fresh-caught tuna, used to make nigirizushi long before they became popular here. She called them Edozushi, Edo the original name for Tokyo. I remember how good they were. Maybe that's why I prefer the old standbys over the new creations (rolls with catchy names) of Asian-fusion cuisine.

Samma (pike) from Japan are also among my favorite fish. Whenever I see the fish displayed on ice at the local market, I cannot resist buying

DOI: 10.5876/9781607322542:c19

them. Once, with my wife at a restaurant in Los Angeles, I enjoyed two samma so thoroughly that I left only the heads, tails, and skeletal remains on the plate. The waitress, a Japanese-speaking woman, couldn't believe how much of the fish I had eaten. "A cat couldn't do any better," she commented as she removed the plate. I let her know that I had grown up in a fish market and knew my fish, although samma was a love I acquired late in life.

Mackerel are good broiled or, if very fresh, prepared raw as sashimi. I suppose any fish can be eaten raw as long as they are fresh. But to me, mackerel is the *sabazushi* my mother used to make for New Year's Day and other special occasions. It is a specialty of Wakayama Prefecture, where my parents were from.

The fish are heavily salted, and after a few days the salt is removed. They are then marinated in a sweet vinegar solution for another few days before being placed on top of the sushi rice in a box to be pressed with a weight (in my case) overnight. Mother didn't work from a recipe and left no record, so I have had to devise a recipe based strictly on my memory of how her sushi tasted. The finished sushi is not nearly like hers but close enough that I enjoy it, and most people who are brave enough to try it nod their approval. I hope they are being honest.

The trick is in the salt, how much is retained in the fish. There has to be some; you must not remove it all, but there is no way to measure this, so it is left to chance. Sometimes it's just right, then the sushi is good; other times it's too salty or too bland and tasteless, and the sushi is not so good. The uncertainty is what's maddening about making sabazushi. Someday I hope to find a more foolproof, scientific method.

I think sabazushi began as a way of preserving the fish. I have heard that in Wakayama the sushi was kept under a weight for many months until the box was full of water and the sushi had fermented. This was called *kusarizushi,* or rotten sushi. I don't know how edible it was.

The process of making sabazushi takes several days; when using hard, frozen mackerel from Norway, which requires a day to defrost, it will take a full week. I like the ones from Norway for their uniform size and taste. When I make sushi, usually for New Year's gatherings or community potlucks, I feel I'm continuing a tradition that goes back many centuries and many generations of my people. When the sushi is ready, cut into serving pieces, and I bite into one, that is when I feel the presence of my long-dead parents, even hear their voices, the familiar intonations of their Wakayama dialect.

Once, when I had a break from school in Los Angeles, I took the overnight bus to visit Father and my sister. At the stopover in Sacramento, I remember going to Father's favorite sushi restaurant and ordering a box of assorted sushi and being refused by the woman who waited on me because it was too large an order at such short notice.

Disappointed, I told the man at the restaurant (I believe he was the woman's husband) that I had hoped to take it to my father in Weimar, and he overruled his wife and offered to make extra sushi for me. I took the box of sushi to Father, who shared it with my sister and other Japanese patients.

But nothing compares to my love of barracuda. It's a shame that they are so hard to find these days. The great ones in the West Indies and Florida are said to be longer than six feet and a threat to humans. The ones I'm familiar with from the Pacific Ocean are tamer and smaller— about two to three feet in length. They are like pike, narrow and long, though much bigger. Basted with homemade teriyaki sauce and char- coal broiled, they are extremely good. I remember my mother cooking them outdoors on a makeshift grill over coals made by burning the boards of empty fish boxes behind our store in Loomis. Besides being tasty, barracuda have few small bones to worry about.

The flesh of barracuda is also the main ingredient for *kamaboko*, a Japanese fishcake. Fish meat is ground and a paste, made with water and cornstarch, is molded into a half cylinder on a piece of board. This is then steamed until done. Red or green food coloring makes the cakes attractive accents on a platter of food, especially for New Year's Day.

Whenever my wife, Sadako, and I have kamaboko—usually in soups but sometimes sliced with soy sauce—invariably we remember how she, as a ten-year-old, helped with her mother's enterprise in Tule Lake when we were incarcerated during World War II. My wife tells me that her mother and a few of her friends made kamaboko and sake and sold them. My wife's part in the enterprise was to buy the barracuda at the co-op store at the far end of camp, run by Issei and Nissei in camp. She remembers going many blocks pulling a red wagon; she doesn't know how she got the wagon, but the picture of her pulling the red wagon loaded with fish back to the welcoming ladies is vivid in her mind.

When Sadako returned with the barracuda, her mother and her partners went right to work preparing fillets of the fish, which were mashed in a *suribachi*, or earthenware mortar. This pasty dough was then molded into shape on a thin two-by-six-inch board. The raw kamaboko were painted and placed in a pot to steam on the potbellied, coal-burning stove furnished for each apartment. Once cooled, the kamaboko were ready for the eagerly waiting customers.

Though essential in soups and salads, kamaboko is a favorite accompaniment to sake. Mother-in-law made and sold them both in camp. In fact, her cottage industry began by brewing sake, which she sold to thirsty men by the glass; when the men asked for something to go with the sake, she decided she would start making kamaboko.

I owe my wife for many of these memories, especially the details about her parents, whom I remember fondly. Such memories have bonded our relationship as man and wife. I remembered her as a young girl in Tule Lake when we met again in the 1950s at the Buddhist temple in Berkeley. From the beginning my wife and I felt comfortable, natural with each other. There was nothing to prove, nothing to hide, we were at ease with each other. That is what drew me to her and her to me. Today, something will trigger a memory and we tell the story, no matter how many times we have told it or heard it before.

For example, we often have fish for dinner, mostly salmon or mackerel, which are rich in Omega 3. Sometimes I get a treat of raw tuna, albacore, or halibut (*hirame*), which I enjoy as sashimi. My wife is not keen about sashimi; she eats it sparingly, if at all. But whenever we have sashimi, she is reminded that her mother used to buy tuna from Saburo Goto of Penryn, who peddled fish to farmers after the war. Her father, a drinker, loved sashimi, especially with sake; but he didn't insist that the children, who were squeamish about raw fish, eat the sashimi. Instead, he had their mother fix fried bologna for them.

Or, whenever we have turkey for dinner, my wife remembers that her mother always roasted two huge turkeys for Thanksgiving. Since the turkeys were brought to the table cut up with four drumsticks, her brother thought a turkey had four legs.

Then I would tell about how my father shot quails and we would build a fire and grill the quails with homemade teriyaki sauce and how good the quail was, bones and all.

Then my wife would remember that her mother always made turkey hash with leftover turkey, how she ground the turkey with extenders like potatoes, carrots, and onions. Issei were great extenders, especially during the Great Depression.

Then I would remember when I was a poor student at UC Berkeley and a couple, also students and poor, was appalled that I would eat half a pound of hamburger all at once . . .

So on it goes with my wife and me, regarding fish or not, memories of good times and bad times too.

Kashiwagi self-portrait, 1953

Kashiwagi reading at the second Tule Lake Pilgrimage, 1975

Kashiwagi performing in *Mondai Wa Akira* with Terry Terauchi at
Union Church in Los Angeles, circa 1978

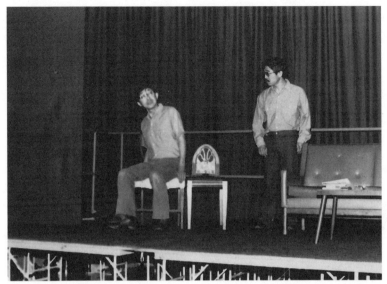

Kashiwagi (*left*) performing with Jim Hirabayashi in *Plums Can Wait* at San Jose City College, circa 1979

Kashiwagi testifies at the Presidential Commission on Wartime Relocation and Internment of Civilians, Golden Gate University, 1981. Photo by Isago Isao Tanaka

Kashiwagi on the poster of the Asian American Theater Company's 1985 production of Warren Kubota's play, *Zatoichi Superstar*. Reprinted with permission by the Asian American Theater Company.

Kashiwagi with wife, Sadako, at a *Swimming in the American* reading, Japanese Culture and Community Center of Northern California, circa 2005

Hiroshi Kashiwagi reading at the 2008 Tule Lake Pilgrimage. Photo by Hiroshi Shimizu

Kashiwagi (*right*) performing with Tim Yamamura in Kerwin Berk's *The Virtues of Corned Beef Hash*, 2010. Photo by Noriko Matsuba

Kashiwagi at the Tule Lake Memorial, Washington, DC, circa 2011

Tule Lake Revisited

I often wonder were it not for young people's interest in Japanese American history, I would have thought about camp, much less spoken publicly and openly about my personal experiences during World War II. When I was first asked to speak about my camp experience, my thought was to decline; but the students' genuine, enthusiastic interest changed my mind. I felt obliged to share my experience with them, even though I knew I would have to reveal the fact that I was a No-No Boy, something I had always kept to myself. But I felt flattered that they were asking, which was probably what moved me to accept the invitation—that plus the fact that I have always enjoyed speaking in public.

It started when I spoke to Nikkei students at UC Berkeley in December 1974. The following February, I participated in a forum on the camp experience in San Francisco. Then I was asked to be a guest speaker at the second Tule Lake Pilgrimage, in April 1975.

Going on the second pilgrimage—my first return to Tule Lake—was very emotional and significant for me. I was sharing the journey with young students who were about the same age I had been when I was sent there thirty years before. We traveled by bus at night. During the six-hour ride I was moved to write the poem "A Meeting at Tule Lake," which describes my journey—accompanied by the college students—

DOI: 10.5876/9781607322542.c20

back to the site where I had been incarcerated. The poem also recounts the history of Tule Lake, the life and events of the time during which we were confined there.

As a member of the Tule Lake Committee, I have attended many meetings with National Park Service staff regarding the preservation of the prison, one of the few buildings still standing. As an inmate of the camp, I had never been near the prison. Now, I have been inside the tiny quarters many times, and each time I can sense the suffering of the people who were held there, many without charge. It is a sad reminder of the injustice and cruelty of the authorities and the terrible suffering of the incarcerated.

Through the years, I have participated in numerous pilgrimages. In fact, I seem to find my way back to Tule Lake for some reason every two years or so. Some of the luster of the early events has vanished, but I have nonetheless been going as living proof of what happened at Tule Lake. I usually participate as discussion leader. I am also able to share my writings about the camp experience with those who lived it and with those who are eager to learn about it.

I should explain the discrepancy in the spelling—the town is one word, "Tulelake"; the World War II camp, named for the dry lake bed where it was situated, is "Tule Lake."

One of the events the Tule Lake Committee arranged and that I participated in was an educational forum for schoolteachers in the Tulelake area. This was a few years ago. I was with a group conducting a teacher training session on the internment of Japanese Americans during World War II for a group of interested high school teachers from school districts in the area.

One night we had dinner at Captain Jack's Restaurant in Tulelake, and I learned a new bit of history about the area. Captain Jack was the name of the famous Modoc Indian leader who led his tribe against the US Army during the 1872–73 Modoc War. From his stronghold along the shores of Tule Lake—rugged, uneven terrain and caves formed the ancient lava flows—Captain Jack and his tribe fought off the US troops. This was the only major Indian war fought in California and the only Indian war in which a general was killed. Captain Jack was forced to surrender on June 1, 1873, thus ending the Modoc War. He was later hanged.

At the restaurant, we met a woman who claimed that she and her family owned Horse Collar Mountain, renamed Abalone Mountain by the Japanese in camp during World War II. How could anyone own Abalone Mountain? When we were incarcerated there, Abalone Mountain was a source of solace and comfort and hope. Certainly, it belonged to us while we were there. It's a landmark of the Tule Lake area, it and Castle Rock. If they belong to anyone, it should be the American Indians who have lived there for thousands of years.

In a holiday mood, I was enjoying an enormous prime rib dinner (probably bad for my gout) when I heard that someone out front had played baseball at the Tule Lake camp.

Instantly, my mind harked back over fifty years to a game between the Tule Lake All-Stars and the Klamath Falls Pelicans, a Caucasian team from outside the camp. Playing and watching baseball is another of the positive memories I have from my time at Tule Lake.

My brother, Ryo, played third base for the All-Stars in that game. He was a slugger and a fan favorite. Whenever he came to bat, the fans shouted "Home run!" Ryo didn't disappoint them, as he hit quite a few.

Practically the entire camp had come out to see the game. We didn't know what to expect; these were semi-pro players from Klamath Falls. But it soon became apparent that our players were more practiced and

skillful than the visiting band of weekend players. Our players probably had more time to practice, since they were confined in a concentration camp.

The All-Stars scored early and often, and by the fifth or sixth inning
they were far ahead. The score was 16–2 when a horrendous dust storm
hit, forcing us to run for cover. The game had to be canceled.

So I went out to meet this person from the past. They were a four-
some—he, his wife, and another couple, all friendly and warm. I told
him I remembered the game well, and he assumed that I had played
against him. That would have made a good story, but I had only been
a spectator.

He said he played first base, and I remembered a Babe Ruth–like
player—big body and piano legs. I mentioned how good he looked, as
though he could still play, plus he was still big. He was pleased. "But
you were all big compared to our players," I said, which provoked a
hearty laugh from the group.

He remembered that he had a great time at the game, and I was
glad to hear that. I didn't dare mention who had won or the score or
the terrible dust storm that made it impossible to continue the game
or the matter of our being unjustly incarcerated in the middle of the
desert during wartime. I just didn't want to cloud his memory or spoil
the magical encounter over half a century later. I wanted it to remain a
warm reunion, remembering the game at Tule Lake. I suppose not all
my memories of Tule Lake have been bad.

What It Means to Be Nisei

At this point in my life, the question of being Nisei (Japanese Americans born of immigrant parents, or second-generation) is probably better put in the past tense. I feel I'm a survivor, albeit a battle-scarred one. I'm reasonably happy and proud of what I am. I'm comfortable bearing the history of my parents and the sensitivity of my Japanese ancestors. It took a while to appreciate this aspect of myself, but now I feel it in my bones.

I also carry the history of my life in America, a history fraught with so many ups and downs that for a long time I could not fully accept myself as an American. But lately, I have become comfortable and proud to wear that skin as well.

The sight of the American flag or the playing of the national anthem no longer confuses me. And it's been a while since I encountered overt racism; I think the last time I heard the slur "Jap" in my presence was when I was still working at the library, more than twenty years ago. I made the man apologize and I felt triumphant, but, like most battles, it left a bad taste in my mouth. I wish I could relax, but my antennae are too fine-tuned to ignore any slights or slurs.

DOI: 10.5876/9781607322542:c21

James Omura, the Nisei journalist who was victimized by the super-patriotic Japanese American Citizens League for supporting the Heart Mountain draft resisters, said we must reconcile our differences and come together as a community. I'm not sure if this will ever happen, but it has been my observation that we Nisei, no matter how different we think we are—geographically, educationally, religiously, politically, or within our families—are in fact very much alike; there are so many things we share in our common background.

Once, I was among Nisei who were strangers to me. They were JACLers—members of the Japanese American Citizens League—and probably Christians. They seemed very different from me and I felt uncomfortable, but as I listened to their conversation, I realized that we had many things in common.

First, we lived during the same period: we were born before World War II (many of us were delivered by midwives); we lived through the Great Depression in the 1930s, and during World War II we were incarcerated in the camps; after the war, we went to work, got married, raised families; now, most of us are retired.

We grew up in a Japanese American environment—in Nihonmachi, or a Japanese community or ghetto. We communicated with our parents in Japanese; most of us went to Japanese-language school, where we spent many hours trying to learn a difficult language. Very few of us became fluent. Some of us had kendo (Japanese fencing) and judo (wrestling) training. There were basketball and baseball, too. Even sumo (Japanese wrestling) was a common experience for us growing up, at least as spectators; some Issei were real fanatics. Going to see silent Japanese movies with a *benshi* (a live narrator who also enacted all the parts) was also a familiar experience.

But when these people talked about Tenchosetsu, that was the clincher. I could hardly believe them. After all, many of them were super-American, yet they were talking about Tenchosetsu, a ceremony celebrating the birthday of the emperor of Japan.

I remember this ceremony from Nihongo Gakko. Two Issei men dressed in black and wearing white gloves would ceremoniously unveil the emperor's photograph and command us to bow deeply and reverently. Then the Japanese national anthem would be sung.

The whole school acted in concert, as we were trained to do. The emperor had little meaning to most of us, only a black-and-white photograph on a wall, a man looking imperial on a horse. Our actions were in deference to our Issei parents, who revered the emperor. We were more observers than participants in that respect.

What I remember most are the white gloves against the dark suits the two Issei men wore. They were like automatons, their actions so precise and correct. I remember thinking they were just common farmers, but how transformed they were by the ceremony. I was impressed with the power and influence the emperor had over them.

Another common experience many Nisei have was working as a "schoolboy" or "schoolgirl" while going to college or high school. My experience occurred when I was a senior in high school. I put an ad in the *Los Angeles Times* and found a job with a doctor's family. On the first night I overheard one of the little boys in the family telling his father, "There's a Jap in our house." I felt like some kind of animal and wondered what I had gotten myself into. The father must have talked to the boy because I never heard that expression again during the ten months I was a schoolboy there.

In their house, I had to wear a white shirt and well-starched white duck pants. There was no mistaking who I was—a houseboy. I worked hard for my room and board and ten dollars a month: doing housework, child-sitting (there were two young boys), and cooking and serving. Company and parties meant a lot of dishes to wash, for which I was sometimes paid an extra dollar or two.

I learned some simple cooking, like baking ham and fixing macaroni. When I went home, I tried my cooking on my parents. When I cooked macaroni they ate it without complaint, but they were strangely noncommittal.

It was a lonely life; I went to a lot of movies on my days off. Once I was on a streetcar daydreaming, my favorite pastime, and before I knew it the conductor was calling out "End of the line." I panicked and got off somewhere on the outskirts of Los Angeles. After walking for a while, I caught a streetcar that brought me back to the city. What was scary was that it was night, way past curfew for young people.

Many of us remember working long hours in the hot sun picking fruit. Even those who lived in the city went to pick fruit in the summer. It was hard work but excellent training; nothing I did later compared to that work of my youth.

After living through the Great Depression, being poor is nothing strange to most of us. I still find it hard to part with my money, especially for nonessentials. My biggest joy is repairing something and reusing it. Recycling. It's no big deal when someone breaks something in our house; I get to fix it. The challenge is to make it look and work like new again. Most newly bought items I consider to be shoddy anyway, which is probably unfair, but I just happen to like old things.

Of course, evacuation and the camp experience are part of our makeup, too. I was in Seattle once doing a theater workshop, and I had a young couple read a scene set in camp about two young lovers torn apart by the loyalty registration order. It was a short scene, but it triggered a spontaneous discussion that was astounding. I realized that those people had not talked about the camps, that they were venting their deep feelings for the first time. Everyone, it seemed, had something to say, and the discussion would not stop.

Most of us have been trained and conditioned to practice *enryo* and *gaman*. Enryo is reticence or reserve; gaman is to suffer or endure pain, setbacks, disappointment, or failure, both philosophically and physically. Once when I was around twelve, I fell while playing basketball and skinned my arm quite badly. When the teacher looked at the wound, she clucked her tongue and warned me that it would be painful when she applied iodine to the open wound. When I didn't flinch, she asked if I was a Boy Scout, which I was not. Of course it hurt like hell, but she didn't know I was practicing gaman to the hilt.

Enryo and gaman work better among Nisei who understand them. In the workaday world, one learns quickly that there's no place for wimpy behavior. When I was working as a librarian, I had a supervisor with a reputation for intimidating her staff, especially males. I decided that she wasn't going to emasculate me, as she had done to the others. But one day she questioned my attitude and we got into an argument, which she, of course, won. By that point, enryo was out the window and I was far from thinking about gaman.

There was a dying potted plant in our office, which the supervisor would not discard and which was a constant eyesore to me. After I lost the quarrel, I yanked the plant out of the pot and flung it into the wastebasket. The story traveled quickly throughout the three floors of the main library, then went out to all twenty-seven branches in the system. After that the woman and I were civil, even respectful, to each other. But the story of the feisty Asian and his encounter with the Dragon Lady—that I have not been able to live down to this day.

We who are Nisei know who we are. Most of us have a Japanese face and name. Even now, there is something Japanese about us—intriguing, even mysterious to others. We have in our time been the objects of others' curiosity, to put it mildly.

But sadly, the Nisei are a dying generation. My classmate Chizuko Mary Yokota Sakaishi (a girl with many names) recently sent me a copy of our third-grade class photograph, dated 1931. In the class of thirty-eight, twenty-four of us were Nisei—seventeen boys, all wearing overalls, the style of the day, and seven girls. Of the boys, four of us—Yutaka, James, Mits, and myself—are still alive. I feel fortunate to be one of the survivors. I have lost track of the girls. I should ask Mary about them. Tell me, Mary, that you are not the lone survivor; you can't be, there are so few of us left. In the photograph we all look very serious, but in reality we were a fun-loving, mischievous bunch of kids. Who will remember that? Who will remember us?

The Funeral

No matter how long I have been away from Loomis, I still scan the obituary section of the *Nichi Bei*. As the firstborn in the family and the only one living reasonably close to our hometown, I am responsible for attending the funerals of my father's former friends and acquaintances. Even though most of them are gone, it's a habit I still have.

It is customary to bring *koden*, or an offering of money, to the family of the deceased. Originally, this was incense money, but today it helps defray the high cost of the funeral. It is a kind of insurance policy because all the money given will eventually be returned. Of course, I don't go to all the funerals, even though Father, as a merchant, had relationships with practically everyone in the community.

The funeral record book, with the names of those who came to Father's funeral and the amount of offering received, determines my course of action whenever there is a death in Loomis. If the offering was small, I wire a routine message of condolence. If I miss the news or learn of it later, I send a sympathy card, usually one I compose myself, along with the offering. Sometimes, depending on who has died or whether I still know any of the survivors, I add a few extra dollars to make up for my oversight and delay or for the inflation since

DOI: 10.5876/9781607322542:c22

my father's death. If the amount the individual gave was large or if the offering was a funeral wreath, especially with the donor's name in bold Chinese characters and topped with a dove in flight—also duly noted in the record book—then I am obliged to take the day off and drive the 100 miles to pay my respects to the deceased and bring the offering in person.

When someone like Nomura-san dies, there is no question that I must quickly drive to the house, where I or someone else from the family is expected. At first it is awkward and almost painful, bowing and muttering lame words of comfort to Nomura-san's widow and shaking hands with the boys, knowing how neglectful I have been.

Then I'm inside, where the smell of vegetables cooked with mushrooms and the woody perfume of incense tell me that death has indeed preceded me. I look at the photograph placed in the center of the black lacquered shrine and I hardly recognize Nomura-san, whose face is puffy, the eyes half closed, and the mouth a thin, wavering line.

He had always seemed old to me, but how changed he was from the cheerful man in an undershirt who used to greet us warmly whenever Father and I stopped for a visit. After seating us on nail keg stools around the round table, Nomura-san would turn up the kerosene lamp. From somewhere he would produce glasses that, again like magic, he would fill with bright red wine.

"It's good this time," he would say, putting the burlap-covered jug under the table. "Only, let it set awhile." Then, calling out to the kitchen, he would order his busy wife to bring "wine-food" and "some candy for the boy."

Nomura-san and Father came from the same Wakayama town in Japan, so they were close countrymen in America, where neither had any relatives. But once, after an argument, Nomura-san stopped coming to our store. In fact, Father was outraged to see him entering the American grocery, and we did not go to his house for a long time. Yet whenever there was an illness in our family, Nomura-san was the first to come, bearing a live rooster or hen stuffed in a gunny sack.

I lit the incense, waved out the flame, and planted the smoking stick in the ash-filled bronze bowl. With the *juzu* beads around my hands, I bowed and repeated the Buddha's Holy Name: Namu Amida Butsu. Namu Amida Butsu.

Then Nomura-san's son Todd—whom I remembered from childhood—nervously introduced me to his wife and sisters-in-law and two solemn-faced nephews. Afterward, I was ushered into the kitchen to join other friends and relatives from out of town at supper, which had been prepared by the neighbor women, who hovered in the background. The talk at the table was polite and tentative. The traditional food of mourning—tofu, tangle seaweed, bamboo shoots, carrots, radishes, burdock roots—all tasted faintly of mushroom. I also enjoyed the rice balls, dotted with black sesame seeds, and the green tea.

After the meal, I went to the back porch to get some fresh air while the women bustled in and out of the adjoining bathroom. Todd, a hulking figure sadly trapped in a dark suit that smelled of moth balls, came to me holding a wide black tie, which reminded me of my boyhood necktie. I had been fond of that yellow tie, with smears of red that looked like accidents, and had worn it on every dress-up occasion. Later, I learned that it had passed through several families before coming to me as a graduation gift.

"How do you tie this thing?" Todd asked.

THE FUNERAL

"Well, I can tie my own, but . . ." I said, turning up the stiff collar of his new white shirt. While I struggled with the tie, I thought back to the days when we were kids, how Todd used to trick me into his bedroom, then stand outside and hold the door, ignoring my pleas to let me out until I cried and screamed.

Nomura-san's widow called me by my father's name and then laughed at her mistake, quickly covering her mouth with her bony hand.

"I'm sorry," she said, bowing.

"That's quite all right."

"I seem to have lost all sense of time," she said, shaking her head. "But it does seem like old times," she said, suddenly remembering that she had been on her way to the bathroom.

"Make me a small knot like yours," Todd said.

When I drove up to the Placer Buddhist Church, the yard was already crowded with cars, so I parked along the street a short distance away. As I walked up, I noticed the year, 1911, carved into the building's upper facade, and I remembered always noticing it when I came to the temple as a boy. I went up the dozen or so steps and crossed under the huge bronze bell.

The front doors were open, and the chapel was crowded. Leaving my offering envelope with the reception committee at the entrance, I walked down the center aisle looking for a seat. Halfway down to the left, I found a couple of vacant places and sat down. There were people I knew all around, and I tried to avoid looking directly into their faces. The Nomura family occupied the first two rows to the right. The next row was left vacant, either in deference to the family or in anticipation of more relatives. Next were rows of gray-haired women. Sometimes I couldn't help noticing people who recognized me and bowed, and I returned their bows and smiled. They were mostly old people, and I felt their greetings were not really for me but for my father and their memory of him. I felt awkward about such socializing and quickly looked at the *gatha* card I had picked up and tried to translate the title of the gatha—"Embraced by the Buddha . . . In the Arms of Buddha . . . In Buddha's Embrace . . ." Then I looked up at the carved panel above the altar and saw that the tiger, with its fangs and fierce eyes and the wildness ready to spring from the bamboo thicket—so fearful an image for me as a child—was only a stolid, wood-bound figure, as tame and harmless as an ordinary housecat.

An old man bundled in a heavy overcoat was ushered to the seat next to me. I recognized him instantly as Charlie, even after all these years. I was surprised that he remembered me by name. We shook hands but suppressed further commotion when the temple bell signaled the beginning of the service.

Everyone rose as the casket, preceded by two priests in black robes, was rolled in by an incredibly tall Caucasian undertaker, followed by the pallbearers, walking stiffly, their gray-gloved hands in front of their bodies. The bowed heads slowly came up as the casket passed by, and when it was placed across the front of the altar, next to the large incense urn, the congregation sat down. The undertaker opened the coffin, fussed with the flowers, then strode up the aisle. Large oval wreaths of gladioli, carnations, chrysanthemums, and stock lined both sides of the hall. Above, the gilt altar shone warmly, reflecting the light of many candles. The low chant was punctuated by a deep resounding gong, and the head priest with the ceremonial fan stepped down from the altar to bestow the Buddhist Name upon the deceased, symbolizing his rebirth in Amida's Pure Land. Suddenly, the air in front was thick with incense smoke. The priest stepped up to the altar and the chanting picked up.

Then tiny Mrs. Nomura, at a signal from the chairman, went forward to begin a long procession of incense burnings. After sprinkling a few coarse grains of incense into the smoking urn, she bowed, then stood in front of her late husband and bowed again deeply. Todd got up and reached out for her as she returned to her seat, her grief-stricken face partially concealed by a heavy veil.

The chairman, a close friend of the deceased, in presenting Nomura-san's biography, couldn't help but praise him. It was the first of several eulogies that followed. Nomura-san, like many other immigrants from Japan, had arrived in this country as a young man and worked as a migrant laborer for about ten years before sending for his wife. In 1920 they settled in the Loomis area, where they sharecropped and raised a family. During the war, he was evacuated along with the other Japanese who lived along the Pacific Coast. When he returned he resumed farming; only a few years ago he and his oldest son had acquired a forty-acre plum orchard. He was an exemplary man—a devoted husband and father and a faithful member of the temple. His three sons were happily married, and Nomura-san's greatest pleasure in his later years had been the births and growth of his grandchildren. True, he drank regularly, sometimes to excess, but never to the detriment of others. He was always a cheerful man who brought happiness to many. He would be missed and remembered by a wide circle of friends in the community. Such was the general drift of the chairman's words, which were echoed by the other speakers.

The temple was filled with the odor of incense and the wet, musky perfume of flowers. Yet even in this heavy air I sensed a rank odor that seemed to come from Charlie, whose eyes remained closed throughout most of the proceedings. His lips moved occasionally, and the Holy Name of the Amida Buddha was audible. I had never known Charlie to be a religious person, but in his old age, I reflected, he must have changed. I noticed the brown Bodhi-seed juzu in his left hand, which

glowed from constant handling. He had always been neat and immac-
ulate, but now there was something shabby and unkempt about him.
His face was sallow and his mustache, always neatly clipped, drooped
at the edges. Charlie must be dying, I thought.

But it's natural for an old man to die; he must be over eighty. No one
really knew his age or background. People said he came from an upper-
class family, but Charlie always denied that he had a family and called
such talk nonsense, lies. His only family was the bosses for whom he
labored in California vineyards, orchards, and fields and the fellow
workers with whom he labored.

It was at the grape vineyard in Lodi that I had last seen him. Even
then, he was a dapper man, slender and stylish, who never missed a
chance to dress up and go into town. He always had a fast word for the
saucy women he knew—the proprietresses of boardinghouses, cafés,
bars, and gambling joints—women he had known for many years.

Now the priest was speaking, directing his words to the family,
comforting them and at the same time fanning the spark of faith that
seemed to ignite during moments of sadness and adversity. Charlie's
lips moved incessantly and I wondered what thoughts he had, what
thoughts crossed the mind of a man whose life had been spent seem-
ingly in pleasure and debauchery, whose jobs had always ended with
the harvest seasons, and whose relationships with people had been
equally temporal. Yet it is the people, what they think and remember
of him, that will remain and have meaning—that and his newborn
faith. We stood up to sing "Embraced by the Buddha."

It was strange, that meeting fifteen years ago. Charlie didn't know
who I was, only claimed to know my face from somewhere. When he
learned my name, he laughed that frightful, harsh laugh and said, "Of
course, of course."

Then he asked about my mother, how she was and whether she was still beautiful, and suddenly a day when I was seven years old leaped to my mind, sharp and clear. Mother was very upset that day, and when I asked her why she wouldn't tell me; she just said "That wicked man," referring to Charlie, the man with the pointed shoes and neat mustache who always came when Father was away—usually on a Sunday when he was at a baseball game—who joked and made her laugh until tears came to her eyes. That wicked man.

"The course of life ebbs rapidly, and those who depart before us are as countless as the drops of dew," the priest intoned. "Thus, in the morning we may have radiant health and in the evening we may be white ashes. When the winds of uncertainty strike, our eyes are closed forever; when the last breath leaves our body, the healthy color of the face is transformed and we lose the appearance of radiant life. Though loved ones may gather around to lament, it is to no avail. The body is removed to an open field and cremated, leaving only the white ashes. Therefore should we look to our future life and with faith in Amida Buddha repeat his Holy Name . . . Namu Amida Butsu, Namu Amida Butsu."

The service was over, and we stood outside while the pallbearers lifted the casket onto the hearse.

"Well, take care of yourself, Charlie," I said, offering my hand, which he took in both of his.

"Yah," he said, and I assumed that he meant "yes" in English, although I sensed a tone of resignation in his raspy voice. His hands were cold, and I was glad when he relaxed his hold. I started to go. "Wait a moment, please," he said and asked again about my mother. I suppose he had wanted to do so all during the service, even as I was musing about him. It was a repetition of the same scene fifteen years ago in the grape vineyard, only with more urgency.

"She's fine, Charlie," I said.

"That's good. Will you be seeing her again soon?"

"I don't know. She visited us last spring."

"Oh, did she?" he said. "When you see her again, please tell her I'm sorry."

"But why?" Then I realized he was referring to their long-ago encounter.

"I tried to make her happy, but maybe I caused her anguish. That is the story of my life," he said.

Suddenly he raised his voice and began to address the people around him. "Please listen to me this last time," he cried out. "I know I am taking a moment away from the late Nomura-san, but I want to thank you for the kindness and indulgence you have shown me throughout my life. And I wish you all the very best . . . Sayonara."

The people, who were usually amused by Charlie's antics, were surprised and moved by his outburst. They surged forward to greet him, and Charlie took their hands and bowed to each in acknowledgment. "Thank you . . . thank you."

Then we stood, Charlie and I, with the others, our hands together, the juzu beads around them, repeating the Buddha's Holy Name— Namu Amida Butsu, Namu Amida Butsu—as the hearse bearing the late Nomura-san drove off.

Two weeks later I was back to attend Charlie's funeral.

Birth Certificate Story

I was born at 9:40 p.m. on November 8, 1922, in Sacramento, California. My parents were Fukumatsu, age thirty-four, and Kofusa, age twenty. Their permanent residence was given as Nankai-ya, a boarding-house at 219 I Street in Sacramento, run by a family from Wakayama Prefecture, where Wakayama folks often stayed.

Though we were aware that the birth certificate was an important document, it was treated as just another item to be kept in the family trunk. But after December 7, 1941—when our lives changed drastically, when we became objects of suspicion if not hate, and when our movements were not only watched but severely restricted—we felt the need to carry some proof of our identity in case we were apprehended.

So we took out the birth certificates and took a hard look at them, probably for the first time. That's when we discovered to our horror that our family name was misspelled on the certificates. Instead of "Kashiwagi," it was "Kashiwaki." How could that be? My mother was embarrassed but could not explain it.

I had been delivered by a midwife, a Ms. N. Yamaura, who made the report of my birth. She must have been from southern Japan, possibly Kumamoto Prefecture, because I remembered that the Kumamoto

DOI: 10.5876/9781607322542.c23

customers at our store always pronounced our name "Kashiwaki." This insight came to me years later.

But at the time of the discovery, our immediate concern was to have the name officially corrected. I was the head of the household since my father was in a tuberculosis sanatorium, and it was decided that my certificate should be the one to be corrected.

I wrote to the Bureau of Vital Statistics in Sacramento and obtained an Affidavit of Correction of Record, which I completed and had notarized by Arthur Flint, the local postmaster who was also the notary public. Flint was extremely sympathetic and helpful, unbelievable in the hostile climate of early 1942. After this transaction, he was our friend. As it turned out, he was our only Caucasian friend when we left for camp. He brought our mail to the Arboga Assembly Center in Marysville. When I sent him a copy of our camp newspaper, he wrote to thank me and to commend me for being on the newspaper staff.

Now to the camp years at Tule Lake. Since I refused to register, I was held back in camp, which became Tule Lake Segregation Center for the so-called disloyals. What followed was all downhill—strikes, riots, martial law, tanks, tear gas, arrests, stockade, prison within a prison, pressure groups, threats, violence, and finally the renunciation of citizenship.

But in the months after the renunciation, I couldn't get over a strange feeling of emptiness and a nagging doubt about what I had done. Soon I joined others who had renounced to form the Tule Lake Defense Committee to seek ways to cancel the renunciation.

Around this time, July 1945, I met Wayne M. Collins, an attorney from San Francisco; he was at Tule Lake to oversee the closure of the stockade but soon took an interest in our cause. At first I did not trust

BIRTH CERTIFICATE STORY

154

him; I could not believe a Caucasian would be concerned about us. But Collins convinced me of his sincerity and further impressed upon me the gravity of the renunciation. He offered his help in getting our citizenship back and became our attorney. In September 1945 I sent a letter to the Honorable Edward J. Ennis requesting cancellation of my renunciation.

So began the process of recovering my citizenship. Wayne Collins spent twenty-three years on our behalf. This dedicated civil rights attorney and fearless champion of democracy was forced to enter individual suits for each of the 5,000 renunciants. Before the case was completely closed in 1968, he and his staff had prepared and filed over 10,000 affidavits.

I dedicated my first book, *Swimming in the American*, to this great man, a man to whom I owe so much. The dedication reads: "To the memory of Wayne M. Collins who rescued me as an American and restored my faith in America."

On May 20, 1959, Attorney General William P. Rogers publicly admitted the mistake made by the US government and restored our citizenship.

So I was aware that my citizenship had been restored. I must have read the newspaper account in 1959. But I was never sure, since I had not seen any official word from the government. I had also forgotten that I was forced to give up my birth certificate at the time of renunciation. The entire episode was vague in my mind, a kind of mystery I didn't fully understand until 2004 when, thanks to Barbara Takei and Judy Tachibana, the mystery was solved.

In the process of researching the renunciation issue, they obtained a copy of my file from the US Department of Justice, which they shared with me. In it I found a memorandum stating that I had recovered my citizenship as early as March 21, 1956. This was completely new to me. But even more astounding was a letter from Assistant Attorney General George Cochran Doub, dated July 6, 1959, which said in part: "In view of the determination that your renunciation was null, void and without legal effect, you are entitled to the return of your birth certificate. It is returned herewith." And there in the file were the white-on-black copies of my birth certificate and the affidavit of correction.

However, the letter and documents had been sent in care of my father at Weimar Sanatorium, Weimar, California. But my father had died at Weimar on April 11, 1951, so the documents were unclaimed and returned to Washington. That's why I never knew for sure that my citizenship had been recovered.

Even after all these years I'm glad for this discovery, grateful and glad for the help of so many people, and glad to have my birth certificate back in my possession. After all, a birth certificate is about life, about life lived; now, I feel a cloud has been lifted and I am again a whole person, certain of who I am—an American citizen. Had I known all this earlier, life would have been considerably easier.

Even now, at age eighty-nine, I sometimes wonder how I would act if the same circumstances were to be repeated. What would I do if I were unjustly thrown in prison again during a time of war? What would I say to myself if I could go back and give the younger me the reassurance I needed then, with the advantage of hindsight and sense of purpose my life now gives me? Would I change anything I did as a young man back in 1943? Still, I often wonder.

Live Oak Store

Live Oak Store
sitting atop the billboard
that said
"I'd walk a mile for a Camel"
I saw
a man and woman
peeing
then standing up
they began
to fuck
it was the Depression
there were no beds
and such
not even food
only love
on the run
watched by a
bug-eyed kid
who got so tense
he nearly fell through

DOI: 10.5876/9781607322542:c24

the live oak branch
to join
the festivity

How did I come to write this poem, so many years after my childhood?
I know my father had a store—a fish market/grocery store—in a rick-
ety old building, probably the oldest house at the far eastern end of
town. It was known as the Jap store or the Jap Fish Market. The building was once a saloon, a gambling house, even a bawdy house. It was
fronted by a wide porch with many columns where horses used to be
hitched.

To the side of the store was a billboard with advertisements, most
often for cigarettes—Camels, Chesterfields, Lucky Strikes—and
behind the billboard were trees. They were actually olive trees, but in
my play *Live Oak Store* they became live oak trees. My brother and I
used to climb the scaffolding in the back, sit on top of the billboard,
and watch the passing scene. It was the early 1930s, during the Great
Depression. The old Highway 40—the Lincoln Highway—ran in
front, and tramps and hitchhikers were a daily sight on the road.

Of course, this poem was written years after my childhood days. By
then I had seen the award-winning film *It Happened One Night* with
Clark Gable and Claudette Colbert as the hitchhiking couple during
the Great Depression. I didn't see the movie when it was first released
but later, when it played on TV. So it was fresh in my mind.

I know that people, especially hitchhikers, came behind the billboard to relieve themselves, unaware that kids were watching from
above. But did they engage in sex? I don't honestly remember seeing
that.

My brother, who was more agile than I, practically lived on top
of the billboard. But he was always secretive about his activities. For

example, he never told us that he used to visit the "jungle," taking food scraps to the tramps and hoboes. Maybe it was he who saw the illicit action and intimated it to me. That's possible, but I'm not sure.

Which leaves the only other alternative: the poet himself. Did I take poetic license? That is also very possible.

No Brakes

The war was finally over for Mr. Porter when he hired Ryujin and his family to work on his pear orchard. Actually, the war had been over for almost a year, but Mr. Porter couldn't forget that his nephew had been killed in the Philippines and had stubbornly refused to have anything to do with "Japs."

He couldn't understand the farmers who were hiring them or even leasing their farms to them, now that more and more of them were being released from the camps where they had been detained during the war. He couldn't understand how the farmers could stoop so low, hiring people who were our enemies. He said as much to Mrs. Porter. "And they're members of our own Grange," he told her. But Mr. Porter was new in the area and couldn't know how the old-timers felt about the Japanese, many of whom had been their tenants for thirty or forty years.

It was, in fact, through their forced departure that Mr. Porter was able to gain possession of his orchard. The former owner had decided to sell rather than try to operate the farm without his Japanese tenant of fifteen years.

This was when Mr. Porter himself was feeling the effects of the war. The war was getting close to him in San Francisco; rumors of enemy

DOI: 10.5876/9781607322542.c25

invasion were rampant on the streets and in the press, and he was beginning to lose sleep and weight worrying about the frightful things that could happen to him and his family if the "Japs" ever came. When he learned about the orchard for sale, he closed the deal without even speaking to his wife about it.

But Mrs. Porter was not surprised. She had known something like that would happen. She only found it hard to explain their hasty departure to her friends when it came time to leave.

At first, especially during the difficult period of adjustment to the new life, Mr. Porter was sure he had made a grave mistake. He had given up not only a secure job as an accountant in a small but established firm and a comfortable home but also most of his savings in exchange for a fifty-acre pear orchard about which he knew next to nothing. The only pears he had known were the ones he ate occasionally for dessert—and they had been canned.

His new neighbors, who were indifferent to his eager overtures, quickly let him know that he couldn't become a farmer overnight, that he couldn't do it by reading a book or two or going to some evening classes. It took Mr. Porter a long time to get used to the feel of the shovel in his hands; the mud on his boots, which he tracked onto the kitchen's linoleum floor; and the merciless sun that beat down on his face and reddened his neck.

Yet despite his woeful inexperience and mistakes, Mr. Porter prospered. It was the war years when fruits of any size or shape—even wormy ones—were money in the pocket. The pears that were windfalls Mr. Porter salvaged, carefully dusting them with his hands and dropping them gently into the lug boxes.

After three fabulous years the farm had literally paid for itself, and Mr. Porter kept telling his wife, who didn't need telling, that the move to the country had been the best decision he had ever made. Marrying his gentle wife had been a good thing, too, for he loved her deeply, even more than he realized, but Mr. Porter was much too involved with the farm to think tender thoughts about his wife, working in the field by day and then going over everything again on paper by night.

As an accountant, he knew how lucky he had been and that his luck wasn't going to last forever. Even if the high prices continued, which wasn't likely now that the war was over, the crop yield wouldn't be as good, especially the way he was managing the farm. His chart showed that forty-eight blighted trees had been pulled up and his crop yield was falling off each year—plus there was trouble with his help.

He often wondered why he couldn't get along better with his hired hands; he paid them the prevailing wages and provided them with free housing, water, and all the wood they could burn. There were those Mexicans and those people (he couldn't remember their names) from Arkansas and Oklahoma. God knows, he tried hard to be fair with them. If they weren't telling him how to farm, they would be sitting down on the job—at least that is what Mr. Porter thought—so he tried to set an example for them.

But he always did things the hard way. For example, to pull up a dead stump he wouldn't think of dynamiting it, as the men suggested; he insisted on using horses. Two men had to fetch the horses first, then harness them, a task that took over an hour. Mr. Porter didn't know how to harness the horses, nor was he about to learn. He kept a good distance from the beasts.

Yet he was proud of his two workhorses, and he liked them in his own way. "Nobody cares for them anymore," he would say. Somehow the sight of the beautiful horses grazing in the pasture not only justified the twenty acres of idle land but also completed his picture of an ideal farm, something he had read about as a child and kept in his mind ever since.

The barn, too, fascinated him. If he had had his way he would have kept it red, but Mr. Hall, the farm agent, suggested that a yearly white-wash was better. What Mr. Porter liked most was having the horses in the barn at night. This gave him a warm, secure feeling, such as he had while sitting in front of a fire in the fireplace on a cold night.

But Mr. Porter believed horses should earn their keep—just like his hired people—and this is where the trouble began. One day Mr. Hall noticed the wagon and the spray rig—both were without brakes. He asked, "What is this? Where are the brakes to the wheels?" When Mr. Porter didn't answer, he continued, "Without brakes? In this hilly ranch, over the hard roads? You've got to be out of your mind. No wonder you can't keep your help. No one in his right mind would drive these things. Porter, we're way past the horse and buggy age, why don't you buy a Fordson?"

When there was no response, the farm agent dropped the subject, and Mr. Porter was glad. Although he thought about Mr. Hall's suggestion, he did not take it seriously. Certainly, he would never get rid of his horses. Yet he trusted Mr. Hall implicitly, for he was the only friend he had in the area. It was Mr. Hall who convinced him that he should hire Ryujin.

"But he's a Jap, isn't he?"

"Porter, the war's over."

"Not for me it isn't, not as long as I can remember what they did to my nephew."

"It's time you got smart, Porter," the farm agent said. "You've been pretty lucky. Do you know why you've had such good crops these past few years?"

"Well..."

"Because Japanese were working this farm long before you ever heard of it. Thanks to them you have a productive farm—no blights on the trees and no Johnson grass. But your luck isn't gonna last forever. Your crop yield has been dropping every year, and you know it. You better do something before it's too late. You better get someone who knows something about farming, someone who can grow real Bartletts, not the puny stuff you've been passing off as pears. Porter, I'm telling you, you better do something now before you ruin this good ranch completely and before you ruin yourself too," Mr. Hall said.

Mr. Porter had never known a Jap at close range, so when they moved in he didn't know what to expect. But he was relieved and quite charmed by the family, all five of them—Ryujin, his wife, a daughter, and two teenage boys. He wondered how they would manage in the four-room cabin.

"It's a real house with a real kitchen and everything," the daughter exclaimed. Then he heard her shout when she discovered the toilet on the back porch. The whole family, the father included, went back to see for themselves.

As for Ryujin, the father, Mr. Porter decided he wasn't a bad sort. In fact, he hardly seemed like a Jap.

"The name sounds rather Russian," said Mrs. Porter, who had read a little more than her husband, when he told her about the family.

"Russian? Could be," Mr. Porter said, "only he claims to be an American Indian."

"Japan lose war, no more Japan for me . . . so I 'Merican Indian,' " Ryujin had said, laughing, showing a lot of teeth. Mr. Porter, though he did not understand what the man had meant, had also laughed.

Mr. Porter was immensely pleased with Ryujin's knowledge of farming. "No one in this county knows more about pears," he swore to his wife. Now, if he wanted to, he felt he could relax a little. But what struck him most was the way Ryujin had with the horses. He liked the way he slapped the horses on their backsides and made them quiver and the emphatic way he waved away the can of barley Porter had planned to give to the animals.

"Horse too fat, need more work," Ryujin said.

Mr. Porter could hardly wait to see the man work his horses. But Ryujin quickly noticed the missing brakes on both the spray rig and the wagon.

"What's the matter? No brakes?" he asked. When Mr. Porter shook his head, he asked again. "No brakes?"

"No."

NO BRAKES

"No good for horse," Ryujin said.

"We've never had any trouble, and I can tell you're a good horseman," Mr. Porter said.

"No brakes, no good for horse," Ryujin repeated. "Too much hill, road too hard, too heavy for horse," he said quickly, without laughing. Mr. Porter felt uneasy, knowing Ryujin meant business.

One day Ryujin came storming up to the house. He knocked sharply and bowed more stiffly than usual.

"What's the matter, Ryujin?"

"Much trouble, you know," Ryujin said and pointed toward the spray rig on the hill. The horses were hitched to the rig, the older of the two boys holding the reins. Ryujin bowed again and strode up the hill. Mr. Porter followed quickly but found it difficult to keep up with the little man.

Milky liquid dripped from the sides of the tank, filled with oily spray. Ryujin took the reins from the boy and offered them to Mr. Porter.

"You drive? No?" Ryujin spat out the words, plain and fair. When the boss made no movement, Ryujin quickly jumped up on the rig.

"Be careful, Papa; remember what happened this morning," the younger of the boys said.

Holding the reins with one hand, Ryujin pointed down toward the foot of the road, indicating to the boss where they were headed. Mr. Porter, following this silent command, started down the steep, hard road. He walked quickly, faster than he intended, and found it hard to brake himself, almost falling several times as he made his way.

Halfway down the road he managed to stop momentarily. He turned around and saw that Ryujin was starting to move the spray rig, steadying the horses, holding them. "Whoa now, easy, whoa now, easy." The horses strained to hold back the weight that bore down on them.

Suddenly, there was a great white splash from the top of the tank as the horses, unable to hold the weight of the rig, sped down the hill, almost out of control. Ryujin, however, managed to hang on to the reins as the horses charged down the hill; the rig finally came to a stop off the road among the pear trees, far down in the flats.

The older of the two boys rushed up to see that his father was all right. Miraculously, Ryujin was still on the rig, unharmed, and the boy took over the reins.

As Ryujin was getting off the rig, he saw Mr. Porter come by. He thought the man was going to steady the agitated horses but was shocked by what he saw and heard next.

With a clenched fist, raised and shaking at the horses, the white man screamed repeatedly, "You goddamn yellow Jap!" Turning to the pear trees, he continued to scream; now directed heavenward, the angry screams were loosed, uncontrolled, strident, terrible, and finally unintelligible: "You goddamn yellow Jap!"

When they thought the man was finally spent, Ryujin and one of the boys approached cautiously, took hold of his arms, and half carried and half dragged the limp but not unwilling Mr. Porter up the hill to his house.

Afterword

Lane Ryo Hirabayashi

THE GEORGE AND SAKAYE ARATANI PROFESSOR OF THE JAPANESE AMERICAN
INCARCERATION, REDRESS, AND COMMUNITY ASIAN AMERICAN STUDIES, UCLA

Hiroshi Kashiwagi, his poetry, plays, and prose are a national treasure that will prove especially valuable to the Sansei- (third-) and Yonsei- (fourth-) generation Americans of Japanese ancestry. In *Starting from Loomis,* Kashiwagi's stories of the Japanese American experience are beautifully crafted, both minimalist in language and complexly textured. Though the stories have their own specific merit as literature, I am struck by their richness in terms of expressing a Nisei's (second-generation person's) sensibilities regarding the intimate history of the Japanese American experience in California's agricultural hinterlands. My intent here is to reflect on these stories from a historical point of view, a crucial dimension to the stories' value, which might not be readily apparent to a reader who has not lived in this particular milieu.

Hiroshi Kashiwagi quite comfortably writes from personal experience. In the prewar world he and his characters inhabit, Kashiwagi is at home in Loomis—with all that "at home" implies. Certainly, a large part of that "home place," as the historian Valerie Matsumoto puts it, is physical and temporal. As such, home entails not just a material structure but a sphere of comfort, filled with familiar sights, sounds, smells, textures, and tastes, all embedded in a particular time and space.

Because of mass removal and incarceration following the Japanese attack on Pearl Harbor and the subsequent fact that resettlement never actually repopulated the smaller rural prewar communities, Japanese American communities from towns that dotted Placer County, though not completely gone, have been radically transformed in their postwar manifestations. Yet as the historian Wayne Maeda has demonstrated, these were once solidly rooted, viable, dynamic communities, even though they did not become as widely known as the Nihonmachi (Japantowns) of their urban counterparts in Los Angeles, San Francisco, and Sacramento.

In this context, it is evident that, when depopulated, the cultural meanings residents once ascribed to their community's physical world are gone. Space, once inscribed as place, loses its content, and our task as cultural historians may become like that of the archaeologist. Thus, while territory and buildings can be preserved, their corollary—the symbols, signifiers, as well as the feelings and affects that gave them their special meaning—cannot as easily be understood or even captured. What is more, the home places of first- and second-generation Japanese American families have a solid but very tacit feature, effectively captured by Edward T. Hall's term "high context" culture. In this situation, relative stability and homogeneity mean that since culture is known and shared, much can remain unspoken. Therefore, nuance and implication become charged conveyers of meaning, and a subtle expression or movement of the shoulders can also convey the rationale or ethic behind a message. This is where Hiroshi Kashiwagi's significance goes far beyond his literary contributions as a writer of short stories, poetry, plays, and related genre.

Over half a century after the wartime incarceration of the Japanese American community, concerned residents, former residents, and activists are taking steps to preserve some of the last remaining historic structures of the Placer County Japanese American enclaves. Nisei, Sansei, and Yonsei increasingly recognize Placer County as an integral part of Japanese America; and, along with allies, they are trying their best to preserve the last large physical remains of that world. Books like Maeda's *Changing Dreams and Treasured Memories* and the California Japanese American Community Leadership Council's *Japantowns of Placer County* document the storefronts, boarding- and bathhouses, packing sheds and canneries, churches, schools, and association halls that helped stage the families and businesses that were at the foundation of the local ethnic economy.

But if, beyond its material manifestations, a home place is a matter of language, discourse, and *hexis* encompassing sights, sounds, tastes, smells, and touch, we have to capture somehow all that as part of the complex we seek to preserve. The issue at hand here has to do with the nature of Japanese American culture, not in the broad, anthropological sense but in the sense of a specific regionalized, rural expression of a larger complex. While there is no doubt that the preservation and presentation of historically significant sites are of critical importance, the fact is that they provide only one dimension of the *assemblage* that makes up the phenomenon of a home place.

Fortunately, this cultural world is still retrievable, although with the passing of the Nisei generation it is slipping slowly from our grasp. Oral histories are certainly an important component of this preservation, and fortunately we have groups like the Florin Chapter of the Japanese American Citizens League that have striven to do this in the Sacramento area. Historical photographs may be of utility as well, in terms of getting at the physical aesthetics of the home place: its motifs, textures, and colors. (People who know Japanese American families living in the hinterlands will be familiar with the utilitarian yet very creative nature of Issei's and Nisei's approach to design, construction, and customizing of the home place and its daily objects.)

In this sense, Hiroshi Kashiwagi's stories are a treasure because they are written in a specific cultural vernacular, set in a particular time and space—the home place of Loomis, Placer County, in the 1930s, when

Kashiwagi, a local Nisei boy, was growing up. Just as Toshio Mori gave us slices of day-to-day life in the Japanese American enclaves of Oakland and San Leandro in his collection of stories, *Yokohama California*, Hiroshi Kashiwagi's stories give us a deeper understanding of an era set in the foothills below Sacramento, one that has passed into memory. Like Mori, Kashiwagi gives us the whole package, starting from the land, the place, its streets, buildings, homes, businesses—namely, all its material foundations. More important, Kashiwagi gives us Loomis's people: their perceptions, practices, and discourses, all the details that might allow us to construe them as fully fleshed-out actors on the stage surrounding them. Kashiwagi's stories, that is, become a critical vehicle that allows us to grasp the sensibility of a Nisei youngster growing up in the Japanese American community in Placer County, as retrospectively filtered through the eyes of a mature adult.

In terms of its etymological roots, the concept of a "home" has roots in Old Norse, among other languages, such that a *heimer* is equated not only to a residence but also to "a world." In *Starting from Loomis*, Hiroshi Kashiwagi invokes no less than a world, albeit a world gone by. Even so, it is a world he has carried with him long after his youth. So although the Issei and Nisei generations of the Kashiwagis were shaped by, and shaped, Placer County, there is no doubt, as he tells it, that Hiroshi brought those roots to Tule Lake during the war and to Los Angeles and San Francisco after that. So while his life and experiences start from Loomis, he and they take lines of flight that indelibly link Loomis to the wider world surrounding it. Hiroshi Kashiwagi thus invites us into that special place—his home place—to relive with him that meaningful world: a world that was shattered irreparably by the domestic policies against Japanese Americans during the war, but a world that still lives on vibrantly in this Nisei author's heart.